Pushed
From a Train

Travel Lessons
from the
Misadventures
Of a
Global Nomad

Kolin Jeffery Gonçalves

Cover designed by Kolin Jeffery Gonçalves

Kolin Jeffery Gonçalves
Visit my websites:
http://kolinstravels.blogspot.com/
https://kjgoncalves.wixsite.com/kolinstravels
https://www.youtube.com/c/KolinsTravelsNow

First Printing: December 2017

Mum,
Thanks for yelling at me to "go outside and
play!" and maybe, just maybe, for pushing me
from that train.

Table of Contents

INTRODUCTION

Pushed From a Train

*"An expert is a man who has made
all the mistakes which can be
made in a narrow field."*
—Niels Bohr

My sense of adventure grew soon after my mother pushed me from a train. At the moment of flying through the air, I did not appreciate the lesson Mum had in mind when she shoved me from behind. Nor did I understand the principle to be learned when I landed on my knees in the gravel just a hair breadth away from the passenger cars clacking past my ears.

Fortunately it was a small train—the kind you ride with your family around your local amusement park feeling half bored in a lazy, happy stupor. I say "fortunately" because if that train had been traveling any faster than the 10 mph (16 kmph) that it was, then I might not be here now to tell you of that pivotal moment which led to a life of travel and adventure.

I and a handful of my school friends and our families boarded the train at an expansive, verdant, tropical park in the state of São Paulo, Brazil. As the diminutive locomotive traced its circuit around the jacaranda trees and rolling lawns, my nine and ten-year-old friends decided to make the journey more exciting by jumping on and off the train. To accomplish this daredevilry they stepped down onto the running board of the passenger car while holding onto a bench, jumped off and hit the ground running, then ran next to the train for a few seconds before hopping back on again.

Doug, William and Johnny had already jumped on and off several times while I was still working up the courage to take that leap of faith. It looked like fun. Really, it did. But the sight of that gravel rushing past my feet in a blur made me believe that my legs could never catch up to my body's momentum if I jumped.

Then, with typical impatience, Mum shoved me in the back shouting, "Go on, Kolin!" and propelled me into the rushing air just a split second before I was ready to jump. Mum's dubious encouragement caught me off guard, of course, which didn't help my legs with their landing in the least. I tripped, either on the gravel or over my own feet—I don't recall, but I do remember landing on my hands and knees in shock that my own mother had just pushed me from a train! I knelt there for what seemed like half an hour while I overcame the stinging pain of the tiny rocks which dug into my knees and palms. The whole train whisked by before I raised my head to see my friends gawking at me over the back of the last bench of the caboose.

The theme song for "Chariots of Fire" played in my mind as I pushed my injured body to its feet and began to sprint after the little train. The caboose already had a 30 foot (10 meter) lead that I had to make up. To a child, that train seemed fast, but I knew my nine-year-old legs were faster. Slowly but surely, the distance between me and that train shrank in half, and I kept running. Caught up in the drama, Doug and William and Johnny began to pound a clanging rhythm with their fists on the metal sides of the caboose, shouting, "Come on, Kolin! Run! You can do it! Come on! Faster!"

I caught up to the train's tail end, but then had to make my way around to the side of the train to be able to jump back on the running board. With an extra burst of speed I rounded the caboose's corner but soon began to struggle to catch up to the back edge of the running board. I was running out of steam, but the little locomotive wasn't! Frantically, I reached for the leg of the nearest bench so I could pull myself onto the train, but I just couldn't seem to time my faltering steps just right to make the leap onto the train. Someone grabbed me by the shirt and tried to pull me up, so I took my cue and leapt with my left leg raised, hoping to land with my feet firmly on the running board.

When I dared to open my eyes, I found myself safely back on the train. I smiled when my friends' cheers gradually grew louder than the adrenaline-fueled pounding of my heart in my ears. After patting me on the back, my friends jumped off the train again! They left me there huffing and puffing as they sauntered across the lawn to find some new entertainment. What was I to do? I didn't want to miss out on their fun. So, of course, I jumped...and fell again. At least the second time I didn't have to chase down the train.

So what was Mum thinking when she pushed me from that train? What in the world could have been going through her mind when she catapulted her only begotten son into the void? Well, I think she wanted me to be more adventurous. And what better ways are there to make your son more adventurous than to shove him from a moving train, right? There are many. Yet at that moment, pushing me off a train was the opportunity that presented itself, so my Mum took it.

Sometimes that's how it is in life: perfect opportunities don't often come along so you take the best ones given you. At times, calculated risks must be taken, and you will never know the results unless you jump in and hit the ground running. Some ideas work and others fail. Some goals are reached, and others you give up on. But even when things don't go as planned, at least you were engaged in the joys, pains and lessons of the journey. Therein lies your adventure.

Risk and adventure are inherent qualities of travel, too. There is the risk of not liking your destination. Maybe you will eat or drink something that will make you sick. Perhaps you will run out of money before your long-term itinerary is completed. On the other hand, it is an adventure to learn about the people and culture of a new land. Trying different foods is a gustatory adventure. Understanding foreign worldviews and ways of thinking can be an adventure in self-improvement. If you travel well, your adventures won't let you return home as the same person—you will be changed for the better. If you travel well, the value of your adventure will outweigh the risks.

Little did Mum or I know that my future life would be filled with larger, more meaningful risks and adventures than jumping from a train. Though Mum seemed heartless when she pushed me off that train, (She was. I heard her laughter ring out cold and sharp like a hammer against an anvil as I knelt in the gravel.) her "tough love" strengthened me to face numerous life lessons I learned the hard way—many of which began when I moved to China fresh out of college to be a university English teacher at the age of 21. The risk of failure loomed large and there were many unknowns and firsts in that adventure: Before I moved to China, I had never lived apart from my family. I didn't have a clue about how to be a teacher. I knew practically nothing about China other than the Great Wall and that the Chinese rode bicycles for transportation and liked to eat rice. I didn't speak Chinese. I didn't know how to cook for myself, and I didn't have any friends in China.

I learned a great deal from my life and travels in China. I learned most of my lessons in the "School of Hard Knocks." Lessons learned in this school are the most memorable, but that doesn't mean learning the hard way—from your own mistakes—is the best way to learn. Wouldn't it be much less painful and easier to learn from someone else's mistakes so that you don't have to suffer the same failures they did? That is my purpose for you in this book: I hope you will become a better traveler by learning from the misadventures I experienced while living in eight countries and from traveling in over 50 nations. From my mistakes, I hope you will learn to travel well. And hopefully your sense of adventure will grow without being pushed from a train.

PART ONE:
LIFE AS A GLOBAL
NOMAD

CHAPTER ONE

What is a Global Nomad?

> *"My passport says I'm an*
> *American, but that's not what I*
> *feel in my heart."*
> —*David Pollack, author of* Third
> Culture Kids: Growing Up Among
> Worlds

What do you call someone who was born in England but speaks English with an American accent? What about a Brazilian who speaks Portuguese and French with an English accent but who speaks Mandarin like a native of northeast China? What name would you give a person who has lived 85 percent of his life in seven nations other than his birth country? You would call that person a global nomad, and his name is Kolin Gonçalves.

No, I'm not a nomad like the leather-skinned shepherd I saw near Hanasi Lake who tied his yurt to two camels then crossed a mountain pass with his family and goats to reach summer pastures. So what is a global nomad?

A global nomad is someone who lives a cross-cultural lifestyle. They freely move from country to country without ties to a permanent home or job. They love to travel; it is in their blood. Their connection to homeland and family has loosened. For instance, a global nomad might be someone who has taught English literature to Slovaks and tap dancing to Chinese. It may be someone who ate cobra in Indonesia one year, then bulgogi in South Korea the next. It could describe someone who has lived with Kazakhs in a mountain hut, has dined with Filipino rice farmers, and has worshiped with Ethiopians in a rock-hewn church. It might be someone who only visits family once every five to eight years. I am that someone.

Before I chose to become a teacher with a migratory lifestyle, I was a kid who didn't choose to grow up in three different cultures. I was a "third culture kid". "Third culture kid" (TCK) is a term coined by anthropologist Ruth Hill Useem to describe children who followed their parents to a different culture because of a career move. Sociologist David C. Pollock, in his book ***Third Culture Kids: Growing Up Among Worlds***, developed this definition for a third culture kid:

> A person who has spent a significant part of his or her developmental years outside the parents' culture. The TCK builds relationships to all of the cultures, while not having full ownership of any. Although elements from each culture are assimilated into the TCK's life experience the sense of belonging is in relationship to others of a similar background. (Pollock & Van Reken)

My developmental years in England, Brazil, and the United States sowed the seeds of cultural adaptability. For example, when I moved from England to Brazil, I was surprised to meet 20 aunts, uncles, cousins and grandparents I didn't even know existed. I had to adapt by learning Portuguese so I could speak with them. When I began attending the Pan American Christian Academy in São

Paulo, my classmates mocked my English accent and laughed at me when I said "rubber" instead of "eraser." So I unconsciously sought to fit in by adopting their midwestern U.S vocabulary and pronunciation. After my Brazilian father died, my English mother married my American science teacher, and then we moved to Grand Rapids, Michigan. There I learned a whole new lexicon of slang and became conversant in the pre-teen culture of TV shows, movie actors, and fast food restaurants. All this is in addition to the anguish of leaving friends behind twice and having to make new ones.

From these seeds of cultural adaptability grew my vegetable garden of values. Some of these values developed from painful experiences that happened soon after my arrival in the United States. For example, some of my peers were culturally and geographically ignorant of where I came from, or they didn't allow any patriotism other than pride in the stars and stripes. I clung to my British and Brazilian nationalities in defiance of my ethnocentric classmates, even though my memories of the past were fading and my sense of belonging to those cultures grew weaker still. Because people made me feel like the "other", the new kid on the block who didn't quite fit in, I felt empathy for those on the margins of teen society—the fresh-off-the-boat Vietnamese kid, the druggie skateboarder, the shy girl sitting in a corner—and made friends with them.

I valued my relatively stable family life. Outside the home, I was adjusting to a new teen world where people were not always kind or accepting of strangers. But inside my home, I felt safe to be myself. This sense of safety came from being with the only person who really understood where I was coming from—my Mum. Security also came from a disciplined home life where I knew what to expect. Mum enforced regular mealtimes, many chores, and rules like doing your homework first before going outside to play and never missing school, even if you puked your breakfast.

Once I became a young adult, I took an assortment of values from my vegetable garden with me to China. As my airplane carried me across the Pacific, I carried within me the approval of all things neat and tidy and organized that my English mother drilled into my brain. In my heart I held the fun-loving, easy-going nature of my Brazilian father's family. I clung to the very American concepts of independence and individualism—values that validated my lonely childhood struggle to overcome social and cultural differences.

My independence and individualism confronted communalism and relationship in China. Selfish ambition and self-reliance were no longer lauded. Instead, sacrifice for the greater good and *guanxi*—an interdependence on relationships, whether on true friends or on convenient acquaintances—were the modi operandi. For example, all my university students were forced to do community service through manual labor around campus. Sometimes this meant digging holes for saplings. At other times it meant shoveling the campus roads clear of snow. Once I saw students helping the university gardeners to plant flowers on either side of the main gate. Students still complained about the work behind their leader's backs, but never openly. To do so would bring a harangue against selfishness and a lecture about duty to one's university for the benefit of all. On the other hand, if you were "in" with the cadre in charge of student activities and discipline, maybe you would be assigned supervisory duty and be spared the brunt of the labor.

As a third culture kid who had already accepted how things are done in two new cultures, I didn't see this as weird or wrong. It was just different. "Just different, not wrong" became my motto for all subsequent cultural discoveries. My mental monologue in reaction to new manners and customs went something like this:

"Oh. Everyone is spitting out their fish bones on the table next to their rice bowl...O.K. Looks quite convenient. Saves me from having to surreptitiously spit them out into my napkin."

"Whoa! Those toddlers outside that clinic have I.V needles inserted into their foreheads while their mothers hold the serum-filled bag above them. Hmm...makes sense, I guess. That way the kids can play unhindered in the sunshine and they aren't tempted to tug at the needle that usually goes in the arm."

"What? Everyone stood up quickly when the Dean walked into the room. I guess I should stand up, too...Wait a minute, no one is sitting down yet...Ah! Now everyone is sitting down after the Dean has taken her seat. I guess that is a nice way to show respect."

"Hey! Why are crowds of shoppers following that blue Jiefang truck? Oh, I see. There are a dozen men standing in the back of that truck with white signs hanging around their necks. Too bad I can't read Chinese...They look really ashamed. I wonder what they did...Wait! Here comes a small police pickup truck behind them stacked with scores of rifles and machine guns! I guess they are criminals and part of their punishment is being subjected to public shame."

In Changchun, China I always carried my camera with me when I rode my bicycle downtown. I was bound to see something interesting or new that I could document. There were so many other sights, sounds, smells, and surprises in China that made life there a true learning experience. The more I observed and the more I interacted with people, the more I learned about the culture. The more I learned about the culture, the more it became a part of me.

Sometimes I consciously chose to adopt a custom, and at other times a mannerism sneaked its way into my character. For example, when a guest comes to your home, you should fill his cup up to the very brim—to the point where water tension is the only thing keeping the bulge of liquid from spilling over the edge. This expresses the fullness of your hospitality and generosity to your guest. I really liked this custom and consciously practiced it when students came to visit. Regarding Chinese mannerisms that slipped into my repertoire, I still find myself occasionally pointing to my nose and saying "Wǒ?" meaning, "Who? Me?" when someone calls. Also, when saying the number six, I automatically hold up my right hand in a fist, extend the thumb and pinky, and quickly twist my wrist as if drawing the loop of the number six in the air. This is the Chinese hand symbol for the number six. Slowly, over the four years I lived there, China's customs and mannerisms became a part of me.

This gradual cultural amalgamation was repeated to varying degrees in each of the eight countries where I lived. The number of customs I adopted was directly proportional to the degree I involved myself in the culture. If my involvement was minimal, then I at least gained knowledge of a new perspective, a different way of thinking, a unique worldview. In this way, so many new ideas and values were added to my multi-cultural garden that I could no longer keep the tomatoes separate from the lettuce, or the potatoes apart from the onions. To fully enjoy this cornucopia of culture, I had to make a salad!

A salad is a good metaphor for a global nomad. Usually, a salad is not made of just one vegetable. Neither is a global nomad characterized by a homogenous group of ideas that fit only one culture. A salad is made of tomato chunks, potato cubes, onion slices and lettuce leaves (perhaps this is a "*salade mixte*") all jumbled together to provide an enriched gustatory experience. In the same way, a global nomad is an agglomeration of several cultural flavors joined haphazardly by life into an individual who has uniquely diverse experiences to share.

As a global nomad, I do not presume to be a superior, self-righteous travel guru with the only correct view of the world. When reading the following chapters, you will soon realize that I am fallibly human in my pride and prejudices, and the stories I tell are more fumbling misadventures than exotic journeys. That is life; not every path is perfect and not every journey is jolly. Things go wrong, but that is how I learn—from my mistakes. Plutarch said, "To make no mistake is not in the power of man; but from their errors and mistakes the wise and good learn wisdom for the future." I hope that from my mistakes you will learn wisdom for your future.

CHAPTER TWO

"Home" Sweet Home

"I long, as does every human being, to be at home wherever I find myself." —*Maya Angelou*

I don't have a home. Or maybe I have eight homes—one in each of the countries where I lived. Grand Rapids, Jeju, Changchun, Košice and Ifrane all felt like home when I was there because they became familiar to me, but I don't own an apartment or house in any of those cities. The Oxford English Dictionary defines home as, "the place where one lives permanently, especially as a member of a family or household." Of course, I have lived with my family, but I haven't lived anywhere long enough to call it a permanent residence. My personal record for living in one place is ten consecutive years, but now I live alone, thousands of miles from my family. So where is my home? I don't know. "Home" is a nebulous concept for a global nomad.

When traveling, my "home" becomes even more ephemeral. For example, during one of my winter holidays in China, I said to my friend Kevin, "Let's go home," since I was tired after a long day of exploring Chengdu.

"What?! You want to go back to Changchun? We still have a month of holiday left!" Kevin replied.

"Oh. I meant the Traffic Hotel," I explained.

Home is where my pillow is. I have little attachment to any abode, previous or current. This flexibility to call any new place "home" makes overseas living and long-term travel much easier. I don't miss anywhere. I can adapt to almost any new bed (or lack of bed) in any room (if you can call it a room) and be content to return there to sleep after a long day of exploring. In addition, being willing to sleep anywhere has given me the privilege of experiencing family life in some pretty remote regions. Another advantage is that when my travels are over and I return to my apartment, I am all the more appreciative of the modern comforts God has blessed me with. For example, a tin shack in the remote *Tian Shan* (Heavenly Mountains) of Xinjiang province, China was one of my "homes" which made me appreciate a soft bed and a water heater when I got back to my apartment in Changchun.

These kinds of adventures are more fun when shared with a friend. When having a good time, sharing it with a friend makes the experience twice as enjoyable. On the other hand, if something goes wrong, you don't feel so lonely when with a friend. In short, joy shared equals joy squared. Pain shared equals pain pared.

I'm especially glad my friend Fred was able to share the shack in the *Tian Shan* with me. Fred was one of my students in the first class I ever taught. His given name is Zhang shi lu, but since all Chinese students who study English adopt English names, he chose the name Fred. He became my friend, and three years after he graduated from university, he came to live with me in my apartment while he looked for a job in Changchun. Fred had never traveled around China, so in the summer of 2001, I decided to take him on an epic journey across his country to *Tian Chi* (Heavenly Lake) in the *Tian Shan*.

After eighty hours on a train and three hours on a bus, we arrived at *Tian Chi*. The emerald waters hemmed by shark-tooth peaks were a refreshing balm for eyes accustomed to the numbing dullness of a smog-choked city. Fred and I wandered the shore of *Tian Chi* in a daze of nature worship—breathing the brisk air, strolling the lake's sandy shore—until we realized that the sun was setting, and we needed to find a place to sleep. There were plenty of white felt yurts lining the lake a short walk from the bus stop, so we entered one and asked about the price for the night. Forty *yuan* ($5) per person for the night including supper and breakfast seemed like a good deal, until we met Baozhan.

Baozhan was a Kazakh boy of about 14 with pallid skin, blue eyes, and a mop of almost-white hair. When Fred and I left the yurt, Baozhan approached us and asked if we wanted a place to stay. I told him we had already decided to stay at the yurt.

"*Dūo shǎo qían?*" Baozhan asked how much in Mandarin. We told him the price for the yurt.

"Come stay with me and my family. We live up in the mountains. I can take you there," Baozhan coaxed.

"*Dūo shǎo qían?*" I asked.

"Forty *yuan* per day for both of you with all meals included!"

This deal was too good to pass up, so Fred and I agreed. Baozhan told us to get our stuff from inside the yurt and sneak over to a copse where his horses were hidden so as not to attract attention. Baozhan said he didn't want the yurt owner to be angry with him for stealing clients.

When we arrived at the trees, we saw two saddled Kazakh horses—one brown and one white, both small and slender, but sturdy looking nonetheless. Fred and I mounted. Baozhan lithely hopped on the rump of Fred's horse and grabbed the reins. Fred had never ridden a horse before, but with Baozhan in control, Fred didn't seem too nervous. It didn't occur to me to ask how long the ride was, but in the end it didn't matter. The ride was glorious!

First we rode along the whole length of the lake admiring the sun sparkles on the water. Then, where a river entered *Tian Chi* at the northeast end, we turned right heading upriver. We rode for about an hour over sloping, flower-pocked pasture fringed by the breezy fragrance of pine. As we ascended, the rolling, verdant meadows meekly gave ground to soaring hills blanketed by stones the size of baby heads. The rippling river became a frothing torrent pounding over camel-sized boulders.

Baozhan suddenly vaulted off Fred's steed and told me to stop my horse. Baozhan tied his reins to the pommel of my saddle, jumped on behind me, and grabbed my reins. To my surprise, he steered the horses toward the seething rapids! Baozhan hadn't said anything about a river crossing. He saw my worried look and beamed.

"*Méi shì*," he assured, telling me not to worry.

The crystal blue river looked like fluid ice. As splashes from my horse's hooves hit my naked legs, I realized only a glacier-fed river could have such numbingly cold water. My horse forged deeper into the spume. Thankfully, the water level stopped just past the horse's belly so only my sandaled feet got a tingling bath.

As elevation increased, the mountains closed in. We found ourselves in a narrow canyon with only 35 feet (12 meters) of open grass on either side of the river. The now scrubby pine forest clung to the rocky foothills, acquiescing to the might of ponderous boulders stacked into preposterous pinnacles. After the ablutions of yet another river crossing and two more hours of saddle sauntering, we arrived "home."

"Home" was a shack of corrugated tin about six feet (two meters) wide, nine feet (three meters) long, and six feet (two meters) high. It was ten paces from the river and an equal distance from the forest. The shiny walls and roof were nailed to a make-shift wooden frame. There were no windows. The only entrance for fresh air was a tin door dangling dejectedly on its disabled hinges. The floor was composed of four splintered wooden pallets laid in a disjointed square covered by a matted, threadbare reddish-brown rug. There was an area of hard packed black dirt just inside the door for taking off your shoes before sitting on the rug. That was it. There were no furnishings and there weren't even any cushions. Stacked in one corner lay the only luxury—a pile of dingy fleece blankets, rank with the stench of horse sweat absorbed from the saddles upon which they leaned. This was simple Kazakh living.

We met the rest of the family—Mother, Father, and the 17-year- old brother Pahachi. It was just the six of us in a pristine mountain valley of the *Tian Shan*. I was not too happy to realize that sleeping six people in that little shack along with three horse saddles and three blankets would be rather cozy to say the least, not to mention musty. But after each day of exploring, climbing, and hiking in the hills and forest around the shack, Fred and I were more than content to return to the shelter of our shack in the evening.

Each night, we washed our hands and faces in the frigid river and sat around the open fire under blazing stars. In a battered tin pot on the fire, Mother cooked the usual fare of boiled dough balls and stringy meat stew which we ate for breakfast, lunch and supper. After eating our moderate portions, we shucked our sweaty sandals, adding extra pungency to the stale shack air, and lay our exhausted bodies gently on those hard wooden pallets. As the six of us shuffled for a less cramped position, Fred and I pulled the shared blanket over our shoulders to sleep. Though my pillow was just a pile of folded clothes, I slept soundly through each night.

On the other hand, some of the remote locations where I've slept have not been so conducive to a peaceful night's rest. For example, sleeping soundly through the night became my main concern upon arriving at a home in Patyay, Luzon, Philippines.

During my two week Christmas holiday of 2009, I flew from Jeju, South Korea to Luzon, Philippines to go hiking in the

Cordilleras. The traverse of Mt. Amuyao, at 8100 feet (2700 meters), is the most challenging of the Cordilleras hikes and was to be the climax of my holiday. The hike starts in Barlig, a small mountain village at 3900 feet (1300 meters), passes through the scenic hamlets of Patyay and Cambulo on the other side of the mountain, then ends at Batad, named a UNESCO World Heritage site for its amphitheater of cramped rice terraces. The recommended period to complete this hike is four days. I did it in two, and my legs paid for it.

The steps from Barlig to the jungle foothills of Mt. Amuyao are impossibly steep. They start across the river from Barlig as stone slabs sticking out from the rice terrace walls like an aerial staircase. As my guide and I left the terraces behind, the steps became irregular, some made of stone, some hacked into the dirt and some were the roots of tropical trees. We occasionally climbed bamboo ladders at vertical sections of this rainforest hike.

Usually, my heart needs time to warm up to vigorous exercise, so starting sleepily at 5 a.m. made my heart and lungs burn fiercely. In addition, carrying all my clothes, a thick paperback novel, my camera with extra batteries, and five liters of water in my backpack soon made the pressure on my shoulders unbearable. It felt like circulation to my head was being cut off. After about four hours of dizzy climbing, my guide and I stumbled onto the summit with no view to reward us. There was supposed to be a stunning, endless vista of countless mountain ridges extending off to the horizon, but all I saw were undulating clouds at my feet that occasionally rose on the breeze to wrap us in a cold, wet-blanket fog.

After an hour's lunch spent sitting on a broken brick wall encircling a communications antenna, we headed down toward Patyay for the night. Descending is always harder on my knees and leg muscles than ascending. The hike down Mt. Amuyao is probably the hardest descent I have ever done: The trail was as wide as my foot and made of slick melted-chocolate mud.

Invariably, on my right was a wall of earth and vegetation and on my left, a precipitous and muddy slide into a maze of foliage. The 4500 foot (1500 meter) descent was suicidal all four hours to Patyay. It is so steep, in fact, that the Tagalog description for this descent is "knee breaking like glass." Mt. Amuyao broke my knees. The constant strain on my muscles and ligaments to prevent me from sliding into oblivion with each step turned my legs into quivering masses of minced meat. When we finally reached the even rice terraces of Patyay, I could barely walk.

The next step was finding a place to sleep. It was already sunset, and my guide didn't know anyone in this hamlet. Patyay is home to a dozen Ifugao families scattered willy-nilly across a narrow valley crammed with rice terraces clambering up the flanks of Amuyao. My guide's choices for accommodation were severely limited, so he thought it prudent to ask at the first home we came to. The man of the house, a lanky fellow with a ragged greying t-shirt and a drooping straw hat, didn't look at all pleased with our request for a bed. With a glum glance at our sorry, muddy state, he begrudgingly assented and gave us some thatched straw stools to sit on in his black dirt courtyard while we waited for supper to be made.

The first thing I noticed was that the toilet was directly behind my stool. The toilet was a four inch (ten centimeter) hole in the ground surrounded by a cement wall barely high enough to conceal a squatting toddler. The sweeping view of the rice terraces from that spot would certainly be stunning. In front of me was the family's two-bedroom brick house, elevated on wooden posts to give the pigs and chickens some shelter from rain. Next to the house was an *alang* granary modeled after the traditional Ifugao hut. These huts are also on stilts. They have a pyramid-shaped thatch roof and, though made without nails, have been known to withstand earthquakes. This ancient earthquake proofing is done by placing a boulder in the foundation hole for each stilt to rest on. By separating the structure from the ground, the hut can shake horizontally and thus minimize the stress of the quaking earth. This family's *alang* was slightly modernized with a tin roof hammered to the wooden frame.

Life abounded at this site. Virile roosters crowed as they chased unwilling hens. A slovenly pig grunted with satisfaction in its slimy pen under the house. A skulking puppy with vertebrae poking through its fur slinked around us with its tail between its legs. Three snotty-nosed children, none older than six, in black rags and bare feet stopped their playing to stare at the strangers who had invaded their yard. Eldest Daughter in a bright red sweater looked decidedly cleaner with a washed face and brushed hair. She gave us a grand smile as she said hello on her way to kill a chicken for our supper. Mother quietly slouched on a stool to our left to nurse her youngest as the other little ones instinctively gathered around her for protection from the two strange men. Father had disappeared—probably to have a chat with friends and to escape the unwanted guests.

Supper was served in the *alang*. It was dark outside, but even blacker in the *alang*. I climbed the wooden ladder and poked my head through the square hole in the center of the floor by which everyone had entered. By the waning light of one feeble flashlight, I saw the huddled family and my guide sitting cross-legged around the walls of the *alang* hunched over three or four plates of food laid on the floor not too far from their dirty feet. I entered and took my place. Our heads brushed the many ears of corn tied to the rafters in bunches like grapes. It was too dark to identify the lumpy masses on the chipped plates, though I knew Eldest Daughter had prepared chicken and vegetables.

As the meal progressed, I began to notice something unusual about the shadows on the walls. Some shadows did not match the bobbing heads of those bending to reach for the food. These shadows were not static like the giant corn silhouettes. Something besides us was moving inside the *alang*. As my eyes adjusted to the gloom, I began to distinguish faint lines waving atop the shadow of one bunch of corn. They looked very much like huge insect antenna exaggerated by their proximity to the flashlight beam. Just then, a cockroach sped across the floor between our plates and someone smacked it flat with the palm of their hand. My suspicions were confirmed. The more I stared, the more I saw. The *alang* was infested with cockroaches. With my pupils fully dilated, I began to see dozens, if not hundreds, of cockroaches swarming over every bunch of corn, peering hungrily at our supper from every rafter and skittering down the wall behind me.

At this point of disconcerting discovery, Father announced that the guide and I would be sleeping in the *alang*. Of course he didn't say, "with the cockroaches," but that is what I added in my mind. Perhaps it was a suitable punishment for showing up at his home without notice. I silently accepted our assignment as I rescued a juicy piece of chicken from another marauding cockroach. The guide glanced at me to gauge my reaction and noticed that I was ruefully surveying the insect hordes that would be our companions for the night.

"I don't think he likes the cockroaches," my sympathetic guide explained to Father.

Father raised one eyebrow in surprise.

"Do you think we could sleep on the floor of your house?" my guide suggested.

Thankfully, Father agreed that there was just enough room for two in the entryway of his home. After supper, Mother made our bed by placing a thin cotton blanket on the wooden planks of the floor and a wool blanket on top. The guide and I each had our own pillow.

Just before I went to sleep, I flicked a cockroach off the wool blanket as the cockroach neared my head. I raised the blanket I was sleeping on and saw another small friend snuggled in the crack where the floor met the wall. "Two cockroaches are better than two hundred," I consoled myself. Then I fell asleep.

In rustic villages like Patyay, there is no division between civilization and nature. Various life-forms still manage to invade the structures man makes in an effort to keep the elements and wild creatures at bay. This is especially true in tropical regions like Xishuangbanna in southwestern China where the diversity of flora and certain unwanted fauna is great.

Xishuangbanna is an autonomous prefecture belonging to the Dai ethnic minority. Though the Dai people are the most numerous in this area, there are eleven other ethnic minorities, among them the Hani, Yi, Lahu, and Blang. For them, this jungle bordering Myanmar is home. Jinghong, the capital which straddles the Mekong River, is also the location of "The Bamboo House", a famous home-stay on the southern-China backpacker circuit.

My then 14-year-old sister Kirstyn was my victim for this particular trip. She came alone in the summer of 1997 to literally circumnavigate China with me. If I remember correctly, my holiday with Kirstyn was a little shorter than the usual 10,500 miles (17,000 kilometers) I traveled during my two-month-long winter holidays. For this section of our journey, we took a 50 hour train ride from Beijing to Kunming, the capital of Yunnan Province. Then, after seven hours of zombie-like wandering around Kunming, we hopped on a sleeper bus for the 30 hour ride to Jinghong.

The Bamboo House was recommended by my guidebook for its polite host, the unique, home-cooked cuisine such as bamboo tube rice, and for the novelty of sleeping in a traditional bamboo house. The house was indeed entirely of bamboo except for the floor boards and the thatched roof. Even the walls dividing the rooms were made of woven bamboo slats.

Just like the Ifugao of the Philippines, the Dai people also have tricks of the trade when constructing their homes. For example, the Dai also place large stones underneath the pillars of the house, but, in this case, the purpose is to prevent moisture in the ground from rising up the inside of the stilts and rotting them. The bamboo stilts buried as a foundation are superficially burned to add a protective charcoal layer resistant to moisture. Similarly, smoke from the kitchen's oven is allowed to permeate the entire house in order to desiccate and cure the bamboo walls and rafters.

All these construction technicalities were lost on my sister and me. We were charmed by the simple elegance of our room. The floor was made of long crooked wooden planks with views of the chickens directly below. These cheeky birds peeked back at us through the slits between the boards as they roosted on the joists that supported our bedroom. Thin bamboo mats covered the bare wood in the sleeping area, and one Chinese quilt served as padding on top of the mats. Each of us had a mosquito net which hung from the rafters and ensconced a white cotton sheet and a pillow. Our window was a square hole in the wall. There was no glass or mosquito netting. It was just an empty space to let in the breeze.

Honestly, I don't remember what the rest of the house looked like, but I do remember very clearly what it looked like under the house. Since traditional bamboo houses are elevated, there is a large open area beneath the home where the hens, roosters and pigs live. Thankfully, the pig pen wasn't directly beneath our bedroom, but the hens and roosters pecked, crowed, ran and roosted wherever they pleased. Walking to the toilet and the shower room was like a farmyard tour since both places were also below the house.

The shower room was a windowless, creepy cement sarcophagus directly below the rainwater tank. A pipe came from the ceiling and had a tap at the end which served as the shower-head. A bare light bulb hung by a wire not far from the tap. It is probably a good thing I don't remember the toilet. I think my memory of the toilet itself is overshadowed by my memory of what I saw on my first trip there in the black of night.

I am cursed with the necessity of waking up at least once every night to relieve myself. It is always a chore and even more so when my "home" is unfamiliar and the likelihood of going bump in the night increases. At the Bamboo House, I had a flashlight, and I was happy to have it. On the other hand, I was not too keen on the thought of discovering some wild creatures on the way to the latrine. Before leaving the safety of my mosquito net, I reminded myself of the domesticated chickens and pigs so as not to be surprised by sudden noises or darting shadows. Then I tiptoed down the stairs and entered the darkness below the house.

I heard the flutter of wings behind my head and told myself it was the chickens sleeping on the beams that supported the floorboards. I turned my flashlight in the direction of the noise to confirm this. A spotlighted hen opened its eyes and gave an annoyed cluck. But then, as I swept my light across the beams and down to the floor, a red gleam caught my eye. What was that gleam not far from the hen? I shone my light on the spot where the gleam had been and saw two glowing red circles. My flashlight batteries were weak, so I moved a little closer to shine my light on the creature.

It was a fat brown rat, about a foot (30 centimeters) long, peering down at me. As I watched the rat scurry along the beam, I saw a second equally large rat follow on its tail. Then a third rat followed on the tail of the second. As my eyes grew accustomed to the inky night, I was shocked to discover that every beam not occupied by hens was covered by a head-to-tail traffic jam of rats, scurrying in single file right below the floorboards upon which Kirstyn and I slept.

Just then, I remembered how Kirstyn had heard a strange noise below her head before going to sleep that first night. "Oh, it is just a hen flapping its wings," I assured her. We waited in silence for a while to hear the sound again. This time there was a scurrying above our heads near the roof.

"If it's the chickens making that noise, then what did we just hear up there? Don't the chickens sleep below us?" Kirstyn asked.

"I don't know," I answered unconvincingly, "maybe a chicken flew up to the roof."

The answer seemed to satisfy Kirstyn and we went to sleep. Now, after what I had seen on the way to the toilet, I knew it wasn't the chickens making those noises we had heard in the bedroom. My new problem was whether or not I should tell Kirstyn the truth. I couldn't decide at that wee hour. I had more pressing matters to worry about. I left the myriad rats to their business, and I walked to the latrine to attend to mine.

I decided not to tell Kirstyn about the rats below our sleeping heads. I wanted her time in Jinghong to be a happy memory, and it was. Kirstyn and I leisurely rode our rented bicycles down bumpy jungle roads, visiting villages of bamboo houses. At each hamlet, jubilant crowds of barefoot children surrounded us, laughing at my hairy arms and legs and admiring the whiteness of my sister's skin. I even joined a game of hopscotch. In the evenings, Kirstyn and I returned to the Bamboo House to savor famous Dai cuisine such as *suansun zhu yu* (fish boiled with sour bamboo shoots), *kao sunzi* (grilled bamboo shoots wrapped in banana leaves or lemon grass), and *xiangzhu fan* (glutinous rice stuffed inside bamboo cooked over an open fire).

Yes, we still went to the toilet at night, but Kirstyn only noticed one or two rats, and I ignored the other 998 of them. The rats were part of the adventure. Tolerating these rodent neighbors was really a small price to pay for the unmatched experience of living in our bamboo "home."

CHAPTER THREE

Fitting In

*"There are no foreign lands. It is
the traveler only who is foreign."*
—*Robert Louis Stevenson,*
<u>*The Silverado Squatters*</u>

*"I am a foreigner, but I like to hide
the fact. I'd rather people be
prejudiced against my
personality."*
—*Bauvard,* <u>*The Prince of Plungers*</u>

He squeezed my knee gently, almost lovingly. This was not the kind of behavior I expected while sitting in a public bus in China. Nevertheless, the man on my left unabashedly reached out to touch someone—me. It wasn't a welcome touch, but in that instant I was too shocked to react. He wrapped his meaty right hand around my skinny knee and squeezed twice. He didn't stop there. His hand slid from my knee down to the hem of my trouser leg. He slowly pushed up my trousers past the top of my long cotton sock until he glanced at my hairy brown flesh.

"*Aìyǒu!*" he exclaimed in surprise, dropping my trouser leg. Several passengers sitting across from me gasped at my copious body hair.

"This man is not normal," the Chinese probably thought as they gazed at my "fur"—the equivalent Chinese word for body hair.

"This man is not normal," is what I thought about Mr. Knee-Squeezer's forwardness and disrespect for my personal space.

But what does "normal" really mean? While living or traveling overseas, you may soon realize that your definition of "normal" doesn't match that of the local culture. Normalcy is subjective.

In this case, the Chinese didn't give a second thought to this man's blatant knee-squeezing because his actions satisfied their curiosity about me. They were curious because it was winter, and my legs looked too skinny. Let me explain.

In Changchun, winter is cold. Really cold. Normal winter temperatures are around -4 Farenheit (-20 Celsius). When I stepped outside, I knew it was cold if my first breath instantly turned my nose hairs into miniature icicles that clinked like sleigh bells in the belfry of my nostrils.

In that kind of cold, the Chinese dress in many layers. For example, they wear so many layers that my female students, who looked like dainty, slender fairies in their summer dresses of late August were, come winter, transformed into rotund, sausage-legged Michelin men who wobbled their way to class like toddlers learning to walk. Normal attire for Chinese legs consisted of one pair of thin cotton long underwear covered by two pairs of thick wool long underwear. These, in turn, were buried beneath two or three pairs of trousers according to the wearer's level of cold tolerance. Now you can understand why my skinny legs looked so curious to Mr. Knee Squeezer.

Apparently my level of cold tolerance seemed unbelievable to the passengers on the bus because all I wore was a pair of jeans and my fur. To them, this made me abnormal. I didn't conform to their parameters for normalcy. I didn't fit in.

In some countries you may never fit in. No matter how hard you try, no matter how well you speak their language or adopt their customs, you will always be foreign, an outsider, not one of them.

In China, polite people called me *waìguórén*—literally "outside country person" meaning "foreigner." Impolite, obnoxious people, usually young men, would point at me, laugh and shout, "*Lǎowaì*!" meaning "old outsider"—a somewhat derogatory term. My students, who knew me best, honored me with the title "*zhōngguó tóng*," meaning honorary Chinese person, for my Chinese language ability and adoption of Chinese customs. Still, I would forever be a foreigner in China if only because of my physical appearance.

I have olive skin and black hair which somewhat helped me to blend into a crowd of Chinese, but my hairy arms and legs, big foreigner's nose, round eyes, and western clothes made me stick out. To most Chinese (except the policemen in Chapter Nine) it was glaringly obvious I didn't fit in.

Not fitting in had several disadvantages. The most annoying reaction to my foreignness was the insensitive heckling I endured while shopping or walking down the street. Invariably, this abuse was dished out by young men in their teens or early twenties. Upon spotting me, they would jab an elbow into their friend's rib, point directly at my face and shout, "*Nǐ kàn! Lǎowaì!*" meaning, "Look! A foreigner!" This would set off a chain reaction of pointing and shouting from those nearby, creating a freak show atmosphere in which I was the main attraction. If I had to brush past the gawkers, there was always one who couldn't resist a mocking, drawn out "Hello-o-o," said with the lilting intonation of Scooby-Doo.

The next most annoying reaction to my foreignness was The Stare. The Stare happened everywhere—on a bus, in a restaurant, on the street, even in my classroom. Before living in China, I never imagined I would become such an amazing subject of admiration. To cope with the staring, I stared right back. The goal of my defensive stare was to catch the offender's eye with an unblinking gaze. Sometimes the person would break eye contact quickly to continue looking me up and down, but after meeting my gaze the second time, they would snap out of their reverie. Because my stare made them feel uncomfortable, they finally realized I am also a human and might not appreciate such close inspection. Unfortunately, I became so habituated that I have caught myself unconsciously staring at people while traveling in Europe or the U.S where this is definitely taboo.

The third disadvantage to being a freak in China was the touching. This was not only limited to strangers on buses but was also done by my students. In Oral English class, I was standing over two students, listening to their conversation. Suddenly I was aware of a stroking sensation, ever so light like the brush of a breeze, on my forearm hair. I spun around to spy Helen (See Chapter Eight) quickly withdrawing her hand.

"Helen. What are you doing?" I gently remonstrated.

"I just wanted to feel your hair. It looks so lovely. I didn't think you could feel me touching it," Helen explained shyly.

I smiled at Helen then turned to finish listening to the other students. I thought it was funny that since Helen had no hair on her arms or legs, she didn't realize just how sensitive those follicles are. I could overlook Helen's curiosity, but being petted by strangers like Mr. Knee Squeezer was another matter.

Once, I thought I would turn the tables in my favor. I told my student friend Beatles that I had a great entrepreneurial idea. I wanted him to make a large poster-board sign with the words in Chinese: "Come Touch the Foreigner's Fur. One Yuan per Stroke." Then I told Beatles he could come with me to Renmin

Guangchang—The People's Square—in Changchun. I would stand in the center of the square with the sign hanging around my neck, and Beatles could be my caller to attract a crowd.

"We could make a lot of money!" I told Beatles. Beatles just laughed. He wouldn't do it, not even for 50 percent of the profit!

In China, the advantages to not fitting in existed only because of my status as a foreign teacher. All teachers are very well respected in China. In fact, children are taught that the teacher is the parent in the classroom. A student must treat their teacher with the same respect they would ascribe to their mother or father. Foreign teachers are even more highly regarded—partly for their position and expertise, but mostly because of their foreignness which students find interesting and attractive. My students also appreciated the fact that I left my far-away home and family to teach them. But, really, it is because I was foreign that I was considered special.

One benefit of being a foreign teacher was my salary. Though my monthly wage of $350 may seem like a paltry sum, this was three to four times what a Chinese university professor would make in 2002. In addition, my university provided a rent-free apartment, so my only expenses were travel and food. Most of the time, even my food was taken care of.

A second advantage was that my students often provided my supper. I arranged this by using my foreignness to my advantage. Since my students wanted to learn about me and my culture and to practice their English with a native speaker, at the beginning of every semester I made an open invitation for them to visit me at my apartment. If any of them wanted to come in pairs or in a small group, they just told me what evening they wanted to visit. I always offered to pay for their meal, but more often than not they took it upon themselves to go to Balipu market to buy the food. After arriving at my door carrying plastic bags bursting with garlic, potatoes, spinach, tomatoes, chicken, beef, mushrooms, green peppers, carrots, and fat, they happily filed into my kitchen to cook a wonderful meal with seven or eight succulent dishes. My only job was to wash the rice and place it in the rice cooker.

It was a mutually beneficial deal, really. I enjoyed a scrumptious supper and the pleasure of getting to know my lovely students. They also enjoyed the meal as a welcome break from the student canteen's filthy slop which occasionally contained hidden morsels of rat feces and insect parts. In addition, my students gained two or three extra hours of private English tutoring while we chatted and played games after supper.

I wasn't the only person to encourage student visits. Most foreign teachers in Changchun also invited students to their homes for games and meals. It was common practice in a teacher-student culture that supported not only the development of English language skills, but also the building of intercultural friendships. For me, this friendship between students and foreign teacher is what set China apart from the other four countries where I taught. My status as a foreign teacher combined with my students' friendliness and eagerness to learn made teaching in China a real joy.

Fitting in is also a joy. Out of the eight countries where I've lived, this has only been true in Brazil and Morocco. This blessing of fitting in was only possible because of my physical appearance and my ability to speak the local language, not because of my assimilation into the culture. For example, I have Brazilian citizenship, but I feel weak emotional ties to the country and little practical knowledge of cultural norms because my short five-year stay as a child in São Paulo was not enough to make me "truly" Brazilian. This kind of identity crisis is a common problem for third culture kids.

As a third culture kid, I don't feel like I really belong in any country. I was born in England, but I remember little of my six years there. A six-year-old boy taken from his birth country retains little to nothing of his native culture. The only British things about me are my first name and my pronunciation of the words yoghurt and herb. I can remember more about my five childhood years in Brazil, so my connection to that country is stronger than to England. On the other hand, I feel my four years in China and thirteen years in the U.S make me equally or perhaps even more Chinese and American than Brazilian because of the degree to which I immersed myself in those cultures.

So fitting in for me has never gone as deep as being integrated into a culture. If you only consider my appearance and language ability, then Brazil and Morocco are the two countries where I didn't stand out as an oddity. For example, in Morocco, one of life's little pleasures was being able to walk down the street without someone pointing and shouting, "*Lǎowài!*" No one gave me The Stare. In fact, I apparently look so Moroccan that national tourists in Ifrane sometimes stopped me on the street to ask in Darija, the local Arabic dialect, for directions. They looked a bit surprised when I asked them in French, Morocco's other national language, to repeat their question. After I told them how to get to the stone lion or Source Vittel, they drove away looking confused, probably wondering why that Moroccan guy refused to speak Darija.

Being mistaken for a local in any country is rarely a disadvantage. In general, I believe humans are more accepting of anyone who looks like them. Resembling the locals quiets xenophobic tendencies, and even when you are discovered to be a foreigner, the national's perception of you as the other is lessened. In addition, if you add to your physical camouflage proficiency in the local language, your blending powers are increased exponentially, especially if your pronunciation skills are native-like. Then you are almost sure to benefit from local prices on souvenirs and food. Because you don't look like a foreigner (as long as your clothes don't give you away) you will not see dollar signs glinting in merchants' eyes, which usually happens when a souvenir-shopping foreigner is spotted. If your pronunciation is native-like, your physical camouflage won't be shattered when you open your mouth to speak.

The only time being mistaken for a native can be disadvantageous is when you have a run-in with the law. Two such incidents happened in the south of Morocco while I was driving my family around the country for their Christmas holiday.

Wedged snugly into a white Citroen Berlingo, a kind of car-van combination, the five of us were leaving the burnished dunes of Merzouga behind when I drove up to a police checkpoint. Unfortunately, I misread the police sign on the side of the road and *ralentissez*—ed, slowed down, when I should have *halte*d. A gendarme sauntered to my window and spoke to me in Darija. When I said, "*Excusez-moi*?" he explained in French that my infraction warranted a 700 Dirham ($70) fine. He asked for my documents, so I handed him my U.S driver's license and Moroccan resident card. Surely he would notice that I was a foreigner and let me go free for such an innocent mistake as misreading the sign. He quickly glanced at my driver's license but didn't seem to pay attention to my resident card on which was written my nationality and profession.

"700 Dirhams, please," the gendarme nonchalantly demanded.

Not wanting to pay the full amount, I took my time fishing in my wallet for a 200 dirham note, then slowly passed it to him with the most pitiful look I could muster.

"*Non, non, monsieur*! I don't take bribes!" he half-heartedly protested, then he walked away.

I replaced my money and waited, wondering what to do next. When my foreign friends had been caught for speeding in Morocco, all they had to do was smile, say they were sorry, and then merrily go on their way. Why was I being charged $70 just for failing to stop at a tiny round sign with barely visible French writing on it? Maybe it was because the gendarme assumed I was Moroccan. Perhaps if I was white and didn't speak a lick of

French, I might be forgiven. Finally, the gendarme returned with my resident card uppermost.

"So you're British, eh?"

"*Oui.*"

"You're a professor at Al Akhawayn University?"

"*Oui.*"

"Well, next time, please read the sign carefully. Have a safe trip."

I quietly thanked God for my resident card which proved my position at Morocco's most prestigious university. My Moroccan appearance had almost nullified my advantageous foreign teacher status. Ten minutes later I was stopped at a second checkpoint just inside the town of Erfoud.

Once again, the gendarme asked me, in Darija, for my papers. When I politely asked the man to speak French, he looked completely shocked.

"What? You're a foreigner?" he exclaimed in French.

"*Oui, monsieur. Je suis anglais,*" I told him my nationality.

"Wow! You really look Moroccan!" the policeman enthused.

"Yes, so people tell me," I replied.

"Sorry to bother you. Have a safe trip," he dismissed me with a smile and a wave.

Fortunately, my foreigner privileges triumphed once again. As I said goodbye to the friendly gendarme, the acceptance of my chameleon identity spread a warm glow of content through my heart and a smile across my pseudo-Moroccan, British-Brazilian lips.

This train in England is smaller than the one Mum pushed me from, but my expression pretty well matches my feelings after I was pushed from the train in Brazil. This photo was taken about four years before that fateful incident. Daddy is behind me and Mum is sitting next to him.

As a TCK, I valued my relatively stable family life with Mum and sisters Kirstyn (left) and Karyssa (right).

With his sure-footed Kazakh horses, Pahachi took us high into the *Tian Shan* mountains of Xinjiang Province, China. Summer 2001.

Ifugao *alang* are built earthquake-resistant. The hut I ate supper in was like the one on the left.

The lovely girl who cooked our supper during my stay in Patyay, Philippines. Soon the cockroaches invaded our meal in this alang.

In Changchun, China, winter is really cold—normally around negative 4 Fahrenheit (-20 degrees Celsius). Here I am wearing my very warm People's Liberation Army winter coat and hat.

Celebrating my 28th birthday in 2002 with student friends at Changchun Teacher's College. Fred, standing at the back, was my student in the first class I ever taught in 1995.

PART TWO: LESSONS FROM A GLOBAL NOMAD

CHAPTER FOUR

Overwhelmed on Arrival

"There is nothing more miserable
in the world than to arrive in
paradise and look like your
passport photo." —Erma Bombeck

Arriving at a strange new destination can be overwhelming. Once you step outside the hospital-like sterility of the airport, your senses are inundated with a cornucopia of smells, sights and sounds. Especially smells. Though smell is often an overlooked sense, never underestimate it or your brain's ability to make indelible links between a particular smell and a place.

For example, after a five year absence from São Paulo, Brazil, I arrived at Congonhas Airport to meet my Aunt Dalva. We met and hugged and kissed a lot, then moved past the usual airport scenes of souvenir shops, restaurants, shopping arcades and check-in counters. As I plodded, jet-lagged, across the airport's spotless tile floor, nothing that reached my senses triggered memories of the halcyon years when I actually enjoyed school at my beloved P.A.C.A or when I lit firecrackers in the street with the boys from the favela at the top of the hill above my home. But the moment the airport's automatic doors slid apart, my nose was assaulted by the acrid, tingling smell of car exhaust from São Paulo's millions of vehicles which blanket the city in pervasive smog. In that instant, memories of riding my bicycle around P.A.C.A's campus, swimming in P.A.C.A's pool and playing LEGO in the school library during the summer vacation came flooding back.

Flashing through my mind came memories of birthday celebrations with my numerous cousins, uncles and aunts all crammed in the courtyard of my paternal grandparents' home, of eating rice and beans with Guaraná Antarctica (a popular beverage made from the guaraná berry), of making tunnels for my Matchbox cars in a pile of manure with my cousin Bill.

These fond memories were suddenly jolted to mind by the smell of São Paulo's smog—a sensory memory I didn't even know my brain had registered. Indeed, I doubt I even consciously noted the smell of smog as a child who probably grew accustomed to that smell after living in São Paulo for five years. Nevertheless, in this instance, the power of smell became abundantly evident once I stepped outside the airport.

I have a theory that our brains record at least one or two representative smells for each country we visit. We may not realize it, but that memory is there, buried in our subconscious, waiting to pop up years later and drag us back to the place where we first encountered that smell. For me, the plastic-y smell of burning garbage takes me right back to Changchun, China. More specifically, that memory was made at a garbage dump not far from the back gate of the university where I taught English. My university sat on the outskirts of the city, not far from corn and wheat fields, and I had to ride my bicycle through that smoldering garbage dump to reach the pleasant, poplar-lined dirt roads that ran between the flat infinity of fields.

Another smell I associate with Changchun is the distinctive smell of a wood fire. Winter in the neighborhood of Balipu saw a miasma of wood smoke pouring out of chimneys and wafting down into the street. The smoke was unable to rise, overcome by the downward pressure of Changchun's frigid winter air—usually around -4 to -22 degrees Fahrenheit (-20 to -30 degrees Celsius)!

When I rode my bicycle to buy vegetables at the Balipu market, I had to push my way through these dense, low-lying smoke clouds.

I re-encountered these smells recently near my home in Morocco. I had to stop and ask myself, "Wait a minute! What does this smell remind me of? When did I smell this smell before?" Even twenty-two years after the first moment those sensory memories were made, those smells still had the power to make me pause so I could let the memories of Changchun briefly pass before my mind's eye. Whether pleasant or offensive, smells are powerful identifiers of place.

So, **Arrival Lesson Number One** is: **Pay attention to your senses.**

So far I have only discussed the smells of a new country. I didn't even begin to talk about the sights and the sounds. Of course, these are so much more obvious than the smells, so take them all in and enjoy them! Don't let them disorient you or make you feel uncomfortable. Those sights and sounds (and smells) are your very first introduction to your destination. It may feel strange to see dogs and donkeys, monkeys and elephants, mules and sheep and a myriad of colorfully dressed people in the street weaving around the traffic. The blaring klaxons of brazen jeepneys, the lyrical call of the local vegetable seller or the rhythms of foreign music blasting from giant speakers at the corner music store may be an unfamiliar assault to your ears. But tell yourself, "This may seem weird to me now, and maybe I'll never get used to life here. But that's how it is here. This is _____ (insert country name in the blank). It is different and that's okay."

After all, why travel if you expect everywhere to look and operate the same as back home? Aren't you at that destination to experience and learn and see something new? I hope you are because that is part of traveling well—opening yourself up to accept the way you never thought life could be. And who knows? You might grow to love how life is lived in that place with all its sights and smells and sounds and tastes and textures.

There is so much to take in outside the airport. But even before you leave the airport, you might feel overwhelmed by the dozens of questions running through your mind like: "Where's the ATM?"

"Where's my rental car's check-in desk?" "Where's the toilet?" "How do I get downtown? Is there a train there or a bus? Which one is easier to take?" "How do I find out the correct taxi fare to my hotel?" "Which kind of taxi should I take and how do I know the driver won't rip me off?"

Please don't freak out. You need to remember:

Arrival Lesson Number Two: Take it slow and go with the flow.

This means that if you stay calm, step by step, you can gradually get all your questions answered and finally arrive safely at your hotel for the evening. A good first step is to head toward the sign with the big blue letter "i"—the Information Desk. Most of your questions about transportation and the location of airport facilities will be answered by the sometimes grumpy English-speaking person behind the desk.

But what if you can't find an information desk and you don't know who to ask for help?

Step 1: Hold on to your luggage and be alert. Don't let that man walk off with your luggage after it has gone through the airport security's x-ray machine! Just because he has a laminated piece of plastic hanging on a string around his neck doesn't mean he is an official luggage porter. You definitely don't want this kind of character chucking your suitcase or backpack into a dilapidated taxi so that his partner in crime—the driver—can charge you ten times the going rate to get into town.

Stand guard over your luggage, take a deep breath and look around. Where do the locals seem to be headed? Is there a taxi kiosk where they are buying tickets at a set price according to a specific destination? Or do you even need to take a taxi at all? Perhaps it seems that most people are heading downstairs to a train or metro line to get downtown.

In Cairo's airport, even before my back pack had rolled out onto the luggage conveyor belt, an extremely imposing man lumbered up to me. He was an Egyptian André the Giant wearing a black trench coat and a scowling face with hanging jowls that jiggled with each of his ponderous steps. As I shrank back from his approaching figure, trust was not the first emotion that welled up in my heart. The fact that it was 2 a.m. and the airport was mostly empty didn't help inspire confidence, either. Sensing my trepidation (my face was probably screaming, "Oh, no! Who's this?"), he calmly and politely introduced himself in good English as a member of Cairo's official tourism organization. He showed me his identification card and allowed me to inspect his name, photo and organization name at my leisure. Slowly my fear of this monstrous man abated as I sensed his good intentions, and I realized that the place he met me—at the luggage belt before passing through airport security—probably indicated that he was official since only a legitimate airport employee could be operating within this secure area of the airport.

Egyptian André waited patiently for me and my friends Arjenna, Rachel and Eric to collect our luggage, then escorted us through security and out the airport doors. He then negotiated a fair price with a taxi driver to get to Funduk Magy (our hotel) and told us to pay the driver in his presence so that he could verify we paid the right price and not a piastre more.

"No matter what the driver says, don't give him any more money!" said André, and then he turned to the taxi driver and told him what he had just told us.

With a wave and a grin, Egyptian André bade us farewell. Perhaps you will meet a helpful man like him at the airport.

The taxi driver didn't ask for any baksheesh, but to our chagrin we eventually realized that he had no clue where Funduk Magy was. What had started out well turned into a nightmarish tour of Cairo's dark, dirty, deserted backstreets. Even more disconcerting was that on every street corner stood a military policeman wearing a bullet-proof vest and toting a black assault rifle. What had we gotten ourselves into? What kind of neighborhood was this? What kind of hotel had a friend of a friend of a friend in Slovakia recommended to us? (Note to self: Don't trust travel recommendations from friends thrice removed. Do the hotel research yourself.)

Still, I had to admit that Egyptian André had picked an honest and persistent taxi driver. For the next 45 minutes our driver asked every policeman, every drunk, every bum on the street where our hotel was:

"Where is Funduk Magy?"

"What?"

"FUNDUK MAGY! Where is it?"

"Funduk what?"

"MAAA-GEEE!" our driver would yell back in frustration.

Eventually he found Funduk Magy. Yes, it was a dump. (Thanks, friend of a friend of a friend, whoever you were.) But on the positive side, the hotel workers arranged a fantastic tour of Egypt, the highlight being a three-day felucca cruise from Aswan to Luxor, all for an amazingly cheap price that my Slovak teacher's salary could afford.

The moral of the story is that I didn't freak out upon arrival in Cairo. I took it slow and went with the flow. Eventually you will meet a helpful person who will calm your fluttering, anxious heart palpitations. In this story, help found me. But who can you ask for help if no one is volunteering it?

Step 2: Don't leave the airport without finding an English speaker who can help.

An airport is a much more likely place to find an English speaker than outside the airport doors. Don't pick random people walking by to ask for help. They are probably tourists, too, and either they won't speak your language or they will be in too much of a hurry or both. Look for people in uniform who are most likely to speak English. These people will not be janitors or restaurant workers or even police officers (though you could try asking them for help in English). Instead, choose airline workers, souvenir or boutique shop attendants and currency exchange clerks. Remember to always preface your questions with a polite, "Excuse me. Do you speak English?" Don't jump right into your question assuming that the person speaks English. And if you already know how to say, "Excuse me. Do you speak English?" in the local language, then use it! I guarantee you will get friendlier service if you do.

Also, try to choose a woman to help you. In general, I've found that women have better oral English skills and they are more helpful. (The fact that I find women to be more helpful could also be because I am a man asking a woman for help.) In addition, women are usually more trustworthy and honest—if they don't know the answer, they will tell you so and then direct you to someone who can help. Unlike women, men in some cultures are less likely to admit they don't know the answer. So, to save their fragile egos from embarrassment, they will fabricate a false answer, not caring at all that they are sending you on a wild goose chase.

Until now I have discussed the impressions and difficulties of arriving in a new destination over a very short time period—the moments soon after your arrival inside the airport and your initial sensory overload as you take your first tentative steps outside the airport. This period is part of the honeymoon stage of culture shock. It is the time period when all the new things about the destination culture seem exciting and interesting. If you are traveling in a country for less than a month, you might never leave the honeymoon stage.

But I would be doing you an injustice if I did not forewarn you of the emotional instability that often surfaces during an extended stay of several months or years in a foreign country. This adjustment period is usually called the irritation and hostility stage. After the honeymoon is over and the excitement of the new culture wears off, people tend to become frustrated with the obstacles of daily life. These irritations include small events like being unable to order your food in a restaurant because you can't read or understand the menu items, misinterpreting gestures or body language, things not happening or getting fixed in the time period that you are used to things happening back home. Eventually, many small irritations add up to a general hostility to the way things are done in the new culture. You might see the traditions and habits of the new culture as wrong or illogical. Some people, like me, don't even have a honeymoon stage. Instead they are initiated into the new culture in a state of crisis as you will see in the following story.

◆ ◆ ◆

I was soon to find out that nothing could have prepared me for teaching and life in China. I was walking into the unknown—a vague darkness that loomed before each hesitant step toward tomorrow. Before leaving the U.S.A, I asked fellow volunteers Jeff, Kristen and Kevin what they knew about their teaching positions at their respective schools. We disconcertingly discovered we were all in the same lost and floundering boat. We didn't know who would meet us at the airport in Beijing when we arrived or if anyone would meet us at all. We didn't know how many classes we would teach each week, how many students we would have, what our students' English level would be, or how much time we would have between our arrival in Changchun and the beginning of teaching.

We had so many questions: Would we live near each other? What were our phone numbers? What would our apartments be like? Would we live near our school? How would we buy food when we couldn't speak Chinese? Who would help us? My biggest worry was how I was going to teach. In 1995, the requirements for teaching in China were few. You had to be a college graduate with at least a bachelor degree of any kind. No teaching experience was necessary, but you had to be a native English speaker. Sure, I met all those requirements but felt far less than qualified to teach at Changchun Teacher's College.

As we neared Beijing we flew over green papier-mâché mountains. I even saw the thin line of the Great Wall running atop the mountain ridges. Green fields radiated from tightly clustered villages, which in themselves seemed to display Chinese communal values: All the houses hugged each other in a unified mass.

Jet lag after crossing 12 time zones was wicked and only intensified the confusion upon arriving at Beijing's airport. In

1995, the Beijing Capital Airport was just too small 1
of passengers trying to get out and the familie
crushing against the glass walls and huddled around the exits in
one great impenetrable clump. Gratefully we all saw our names
printed on white cardboard signs, which, in fact, was small
comfort when we were suddenly separated from each other,
whisked away in different directions by complete strangers to who
knew where. There wasn't even time to say goodbye before we lost
sight of each other in a sea of black-haired people. Would we ever
see each other again in Changchun?

There I stood, alone before Mr. Tian Chun De, my Foreign
Affairs Officer (FAO). He was dressed simply but neatly in a
collared shirt and cotton slacks which was his year-round uniform.
His hair was cropped short with a flat top and his eyes looked tired
and watery—a permanent condition, I later learned. Although I
found his brownish-black dead front tooth distracting initially, my
first impression was not at all unpleasant. He was not overly
friendly, to say the least, and had a slow and careful manner of
speaking English with which he welcomed me to China.

As our taxi sped down the highway to the Friendship Hotel, I
stuck my head out the window and gawked at the swarms of bikers
and pedestrians down below on the side streets. Despite my
exhaustion I was filled with a sudden exultation, "Yes! This is
China!" Little did I know what was in store. The five-star
Friendship Hotel and its surroundings were a far cry from what I
met in Changchun. Not even those first two days in Beijing were a
pleasant memory.

Basically, Mr. Tian abandoned me. I was tired, hungry, and
thoroughly disoriented. When we arrived at the hotel, my severely
jet-lagged brain wanted a bed and my equally jet-lagged stomach
wanted some food. I asked Mr. Tian what the plan was for lunch
and supper, hoping he would offer to take care of my meals. He
never did. Perhaps thinking that any foreigner who comes to China
must be an independent and self-reliant individual, he simply
said, "Buy some bread or other prepared food," and then left my
room.

"Prepared food?" What exactly did he mean by that? What was considered "prepared food" in China? I had no idea. And just where was I supposed to find this food? The hotel food was too expensive for the small amount of money I had changed to *yuan* at the reception desk. Even if I found some food in a market or restaurant, how was I to understand the price, let alone know that I wasn't being cheated?

My Lonely Planet guidebook didn't mention any recommended restaurants near my hotel, so I headed out the main gate. Though it was mid-morning, I found a young man frying some scrumptious-looking food in a wok atop a fire-belching oil drum. There was a line of hungry customers waiting for their meal to be cooked and handed to them in a styrofoam box, but it was too long a wait for my jet-lagged patience. So I moved on to another street-side cook with no waiting line. The fact that there was no line for the second cook should have given me a clue that the food was not good. But since this was my first time in a foreign country I had not yet learned this:

Cardinal Rule of Where to Eat: If the locals are eating there, then the food is usually good.

The inverse is also true: If no locals are eating the food, then it probably isn't good. I did not know this, so I foolishly bought his horrid mush, which didn't even look good to me. I don't know what any of it was, but it tasted awful and came with the blandest bread I had ever eaten called *mantou*. I tried the food but it was disgusting, and I threw it away immediately. The Coke I bought was good, though.

After that pitiful meal, sleepiness overcame me. Though it was now about 11 a.m., I was also foolish enough to take a nap. This goes against the:

Cardinal Rule Number One for Overcoming Jet Lag: Never, ever take a nap!

No matter how groggy you feel, no matter how heavy your eyelids are or how stinging your eyeballs, never take a nap. You might say to yourself, "Oh, I'll just take a little nap for an hour." But your exhausted body will soon extend that "little nap" into a seven-hour night's rest right in the middle of Beijing's day like it did to me. This totally screwed up my circadian rhythm and my sleep schedule was out of whack for the next two weeks! I would wake up regularly at 4 a.m. and felt so sleepy the next afternoon that I took another nap that precipitated another cycle of improper sleep. The best way to get over jet lag is:

Cardinal Rule Number Two for Overcoming Jet Lag: Force yourself to stay awake until your normal bedtime in the new country's time zone.

To help yourself accomplish this, go outside for a walk in the sun. Get your body clock adjusted to the new time by getting some daylight into your eyes. Stay well hydrated and eat your meals at the proper time according to the new time zone. If you feel hungry, eat a healthy snack like fruit to quench your hunger pangs until a reasonable meal time arrives. Until then do some exercise to help you feel awake. Even a brisk walk can do wonders to increase blood flow to your brain which will help you feel more awake.

When I awoke from my seven-hour nap, my gnawing stomach was crying out for food. I could no longer survive on just a can of Coke. I called Mr. Tian in his hotel room and almost had to beg him to take me out to a restaurant for supper in the hope of getting a decent meal. At 7 p.m. I met Mr. Tian, Ms. Iwasaki who was to be my school's foreign Japanese teacher, and Ms. Zhang— introduced as the secretary of the Foreign Affairs Office though she spoke not a word of English. We walked across the street from the hotel to a small, grubby hole-in-the-wall restaurant, which didn't impress me in the least. If the environment was lacking, hopefully the good food would make up for it. Surely Mr. Tian would know of some good dishes to order.

To this day, that first restaurant meal I ever had in China is one of the most revolting that I can remember. Before my expectant, hungry eyes the waitress placed a dish of boiled cartilage; some long, wet, thin, translucent jelly strips which were entirely void of flavor; some bright red spicy tofu; and some questionable-looking meatballs. After doing my best to quell my hunger pangs, the food made my stomach turn. When I got back to my hotel room I exploded.

The next day was decidedly better. In the morning, Iwasaki told me she was going on a tour with a large group of Japanese teachers to the Great Wall at Badaling and the Ming dynasty tombs. I joined the tour at the last minute just before the bus pulled out of the parking lot. I was the only native English speaker on the tour and soon felt badly for Iwasaki who, with her limited English, had a hard time translating the guide's speech about the Ming tombs.

Lunch was a superb feast compared with the previous night, and my stomach was more than happy. At the meal I met Dan, an FAO from Wuhan, Hubei province. I soon began wishing that Dan were my FAO because he was friendlier and a better host than Mr. Tian. At the Great Wall, Dan kept me company and, from his questions, seemed genuinely interested in me. He was also more generous than Mr. Tian for he invited Iwasaki and me to join him for supper at a restaurant later that evening. After returning from the tour, Iwasaki called me in my room and said she wanted to invite Mr. Tian and Ms. Zhang to supper with Dan and us, but since her English was poor she wanted me to ask them. I honestly didn't want to invite Mr. Tian, but relented at Iwasaki's insistence. It ended up being a big mistake.

Dan took us to a very posh restaurant and offered to pay for everyone. I invited Mr. Tian, fully expecting him to pay for himself and Ms. Zhang since I didn't have the chance to tell Dan they were coming. From my western viewpoint I thought that since Mr. Tian was also an FAO he wouldn't take advantage of Dan's generosity. But I didn't know that according to Chinese custom, if someone invites you to have a meal, the host always pays for you. It is expected. After noticing Dan's chagrin when he saw my two unexpected guests arrive with me, I inwardly kicked myself for inviting Mr. Tian. It was my first cross-cultural faux pas and I apologized to Dan after the meal. He smiled and told me to forget it.

Though my Beijing reception was not the best, at least my college paid for my airplane ticket to Changchun and for the two nights at the Friendship Hotel. Yet coming from the five-star Friendship Hotel in Beijing only increased my trauma upon arriving in Changchun. The Changchun airport is much smaller than Beijing's, and for a city with a population of about 6 million there was only one receiving room and one conveyor belt for the luggage. "Either not many can afford to fly or not many want to go to Changchun," I thought. Probably both.

On campus at Changchun Teacher's College, I stood before my apartment as Mr. Tian turned the key. As the wooden door creaked open, I peered into the gloomy corridor. Coming from my deluxe hotel room in Beijing, the first view of my apartment was a real shock. The cold concrete floor in the hall was painted bright red and the white walls were painted guacamole green halfway up. The doors to each room matched the avocado décor and ancient fly and mosquito guts (left there by the previous foreign teacher) plastered the living room and bedroom walls. How nice. Across the hall from the living room and bedroom was a large room containing a rust-stained bathtub, a silver 20-gallon water heater, a green plastic washing machine whose buzzer wailed a classical Chinese tune when the washing was done, and a small old Russian-made fridge with moldy food inside. Next to this room was a miniscule, narrow kitchen and beside that a separate room for the toilet. The floors of these rooms were black with a layer of coal dust. (Coal is China's main source of electrical power, so coal dust is floating everywhere, spewed from power plant chimneys, one of which was right across the road from my university's front gate.) The living room and bedroom had a passably clean beige carpet, which needed vacuuming every day because of the dust blowing through the windows.

The living room furniture consisted of two dark brown vinyl straight-backed armchairs and a matching sofa on the opposite wall. All three had lost irreplaceable amounts of stuffing in the seat so now only hard springs poked into my backside. A large desk with a broken leg supported a brand new color TV that looked good but was of absolutely no use to me with Chinese-only programming. An orange vinyl desk chair matched the other seats in discomfort and, finally, the best furniture item being a handy coat stand.

The bedroom had a small nightstand whose little door always swung open and never closed, a wardrobe with a hazy mirror between the doors and filthy shelves inside, and, thankfully, a very comfortable queen-sized bed with plenty of mangy blankets but no sheets or pillows.

It wasn't just sheets or pillows that were lacking. There were no light bulbs in my bathrooms and the kitchen had no pots, pans, knives, forks, spoons, chopsticks or gas in the propane tank. Since there was no gas, I couldn't boil any water to drink, and I was dreadfully thirsty that first night.

Of course, this problem didn't occur to Mr. Tian as he wished me goodnight and left after hurriedly showing me how to operate my washing machine, water heater and gas burner. No matter. On the way in I remembered a few lighted shacks selling bottled beverages on the opposite side of the highway that passed before the college's front gate. I could buy a drink there. So with flashlight in hand I stepped into the blackness.

Changchun Teacher's College is in the northeastern suburb of Changchun. Far from the city lights, it neighbors rice and corn fields. There were no streetlights on campus then. The roads were dirt and it was so dark you couldn't see your feet if you tried, much less the rocks and stones and bumps that just waited to twist your ankle. I had my flashlight with me and walked safely in its beam. But when I heard voices and five blurry figures walking toward me, I suddenly felt self-conscious as the only foreigner on campus and the only person with a flashlight. "I'm tired. I don't want to be bothered by these students asking me a bunch of questions I can't understand. I don't want to attract attention with my flashlight,"

I thought, so I turned it off. My idea was to follow these students since they seemed to know where they were going and maybe they could lead me to the front gate and the thirst-quenching beverages beyond.

These five boys walked next to each other in a line, and I fell in step behind the student on the far left. Suddenly I noticed him quickly side-step and walk around something in the road, so I immediately copied his action before actually seeing that I had just barely missed a yawning black hole that looked big enough to swallow me. I walked by, gawking at the dark rectangle, scared by my close shave and shocked that there was no barrier to protect innocent pedestrians like myself.

Then the road disappeared from beneath me. With a shout, my body dropped below street level, fortunately landing on my feet. I straightened and looked up to see the silhouette of three heads back-dropped by tree branches and bright stars in the sky. The students peered over the edge of this second hole in the road which I had fallen into while gazing back at the first. The students had heard my shout and were looking down at me but they were talking in a confused tone. I don't think they could even see me in the six-foot-deep hole for they only offered their hands to help when they saw me clambering out on my hands and knees. "*Mei shi, mei shi,*" I waved off their help with my best effort at nonchalance. Telling them "it doesn't matter" was my first real communication in Chinese. It was one of the few phrases I had learned (along with hello, goodbye, please, thank you, no, yes, sorry, how much does it cost? and where's the toilet?), and I was glad to show off that handy phrase just then! As I stood, I felt something warm and sticky trickle down my knee and shin. I used my flashlight after that.

The boys continued walking on ahead, and I walked out the school gate, across the noisy Ji Chang Highway toward a beckoning light bulb shining brightly, guiding me to a big bottle of Sprite behind the window of a vendor's cart. When I bought the bottle it was warm. No problem. I was so thirsty I didn't mind. I walked happily home with flashlight on, dreaming of the Sprite bubbles bathing my parched throat. In my kitchen I opened the cap, poured a cup, drank it down...and it was flat! That was it. I couldn't take any more for one day. It was just a small thing, but for me it was the last straw. Because of my thirst I resigned myself to one more warm cup of flat Sprite before going to bed. "Welcome to Changchun, Kolin," I thought to myself.

◆ ◆ ◆

This is not the kind of experience you want to have upon arrival in a new country. From the very beginning I struggled for survival and had no time to enjoy or even observe the enriching differences of life in China. I had trouble finding basic necessities like decent food and drink from the very beginning and there was no support system to help me adjust. This plunged me into a negative mindset about life in China, bypassing the honeymoon stage and jumping right into the hostility stage. So how can you deal with the irritation and hostility stage of culture shock? Allow me to introduce **Arrival Lesson Number Three: Steps to Overcome Culture Shock Stage 2:**

Step 1: Try to accept the differences and think positively.
Remember when I suggested that you tell yourself, "This may seem weird to me now, but that's how it is here. It is different and that's okay"? This is an example of how to have a positive attitude toward the differences all around you. Don't try to always understand why things are the way they are. Just accept the differences. Some customs don't have logical explanations or maybe can't be understood—sometimes even the locals can't explain it to you. Their answer might be, "I don't know why we do it that way. We've just always done it that way." Accepting this ambiguity will go a long way in reducing your stress.

Step 2: Be patient with yourself and the locals.
It is okay to fail. Every newcomer to a culture has made mistakes and you will, too. While learning the new language, you might use the wrong word in public, sometimes with embarrassing

results, like when I asked a baker in France if his bread contained *préservatif* which I thought was the correct word for preservatives. The baker gave me a quizzical look and, with a straight face, answered, "No." To my great amusement I later learned that *préservatif* means condom. I was glad that I had asked this of a male rather than a female baker. Adjusting to a new culture can take months or even years, so don't be hard on yourself if it seems like you are taking a long time to feel at home in the new culture.

Don't forget to be patient with the locals, too. It never pays to blow your top with a local who you might think is inefficient, incompetent, and imbecilic. No local will be willing to help you or to improve his or her performance if you are angry and accusatory. As in any culture, this is likely to make the person you are dealing with defensive and retaliatory. Stay calm, use an even voice and be polite but persistent. I can't overstate how effective polite persistence can be. I've found that this form of polite nagging is often the only way to get things done. It is like saying over and over again, "Hello! I'm still here and my problem hasn't been solved yet. Can you help me please?"

An example of this is the incident that occurred when I returned to my home in Morocco after visiting my family in the U.S for 6 weeks. During my absence, my apartment manager had visited my bathroom with a plumber to install a new shower head. Upon noticing a slight and infrequent drip from my toilet's tank into the bowl, the plumber decided to "fix" the problem. His incompetence resulted in a non-stop toilet flush that began after the manager and plumber left my apartment. That means that for the next five weeks, day and night, 24 hours a day my toilet flushed incessantly. This raised my monthly water bill to 35 times the normal amount.

Since this obviously wasn't my fault, I did not want to pay the exorbitant water bill. But to get the water bill voided, it took superhuman patience and persistence; I had to walk back and forth from my university's business office to the housing office repeatedly over the next four months before someone took responsibility and the president of each office agreed with the other to pay my water bill from the school's funds.

Step 3: Develop a support network:

When I first arrived in Changchun, I had no support. I didn't know where my teaching colleagues lived and I didn't even have their phone numbers. I knew no other English speaker on campus. For the first week, I felt totally alone and I cried often. This was before Skype and the internet, so calling someone collect was the only instantly gratifying lifeline I had.

Being only 21 and away from my family for the first time in my life, the greatest comfort to me was to call my Mum. At U.S $4 per minute, my two 30-minute calls one day after the other did not make my Mum too pleased when she saw her phone bill. She soon put a stop to my collect calls. The only other connection I had to my friends in Michigan was via the Chinese and U.S postal services. I remember waiting an agonizing month for the first letter from my Mum, my Nana and a few friends to arrive. Letter writing took countless hours of my time that first year.

Of course, nowadays most travelers and international workers have access to the wonders of the internet age—Skype, email, and various other ways to contact friends and family back home. So use them. Speaking "face to face" can be a great balm for the pangs of homesickness.

During that first week in Changchun, I shut myself up in my apartment, too afraid to leave its security and explore the Chinese-speaking world outside. I didn't know what to do with myself. Apart from cleaning my filthy house and unpacking, I spent most of my time crying, praying and worrying. That week I excelled at worrying. I worried about my next meal and I worried about how to teach. I worried whether my students would like me and if I would ever get used to living in China at Changchun Teacher's College. I was in a pitiable state.

Claire was truly my savior. When she appeared at my front door at the end of that week, I was more than grateful for her presence. After an interminable seven days I finally had a fellow

English speaker living in the apartment upstairs who was experienced at living and teaching in China. Claire's pretty smile and her nose stud attracted my attention first, but the brightness of her blue eyes and the kindness in her voice made a lasting first impression.

Two years older than me, Claire hailed from Manchester, England after graduating with a degree in American Studies. She was beginning her second year of teaching at Changchun Teacher's College and to me she was an expert. Yet Claire admitted that her first semester was a nightmare, and she didn't really know what she was doing. She had no teaching or education background and learned as she went along, she said. I would worry about teaching later. My main concern right then was daily survival. My journal entry for Sunday, September 3, 1995 read:

> *Claire was such a great help and I didn't even know that she would be here. Claire took me shopping twice to get more vegetables. I bought nine potatoes, half a jin (catty) of celery, half a jin of huge spring onions, six tomatoes, four medium sized onions, some curry powder, six carrots, and three bundles of lettuce all for only 10.3 yuan—about $1.25! That should be enough food for one week! Claire showed me how to do my washing in the washing machine and how to write England, U.S.A, and Germany in Chinese characters so that I can write it on my envelopes when sending mail to friends and family.*

Friends like Claire are the kind of support you should seek out if you are staying long term in a foreign country. If you meet a friendly co-worker or a local person who speaks your language, don't be afraid to ask them for help. You might be surprised at how generous locals and expats can be with their time and their help. Some of my most precious friends today are those who helped me get used to life in the five countries where I taught and lived for 18 years (see *Acknowledgments*).

Hopefully, if you follow the tips I mentioned above, you will be able to more readily handle the challenges of arriving and adjusting to a new country and not feel overwhelmed. Even better, may you not only overcome the challenges of traveling and living in a foreign land but thrive there, learn from your experiences and perhaps grow to love your new "home" no matter how long you plan to stay. Happy travels!

CHAPTER FIVE

Toilets

"May I squat and not grow weary,
hold my breath and not faint."
—The Squatty Potty Version of
Isaiah 40:31
by Reverend Kevin Clouse.

Kirstyn and I lay sweating on a mangy mattress, condemned to wait out a massive traffic jam inside our vomit-speckled sleeper bus in the thick of a sweltering southwest China summer. We were trying to get from Jinghong to Kunming, but our mud-encrusted bus had not moved an inch along the melting asphalt for the last four hours. After the first two hours, I tried walking to the front of the long line of buses and cars to determine the cause of this holdup. Ten minutes later, without even glimpsing the end of the line, I turned around and walked back to the bus. During hour three, I napped. During hour four, I read a novel. Now, halfway through the fifth hour of waiting, I was meticulously studying every banana and papaya tree outside my window, trying to distract my mind from the growing urge to relieve myself.

I just didn't want to go. *Where* would I go? Sure, there were plenty of trees next to the road, but inside the cars and buses there were hundreds of pairs of eyes that might see me pull down my pants to squat. Not to mention poisonous plants that might palpate my privates and jungle snakes just waiting to strike. Where was a toilet when you really needed one? I wasn't even dreaming of that western wonder—a shiny, white ceramic bowl with a comfortable seat and a water tank upon which to recline. In my condition, any decent squatty potty would do. I would have welcomed the sight of that hole in the floor with elevated footprints on either side on which to place your feet.

Finally, I could hold it no longer and ventured forth to discover what manner of facilities might await. *"Césuo zaì nálǐ?"* I asked several locals who were sitting on their haunches, enthralled by the marvelous spectacle of a traffic jam right outside their front door. Each person I asked pointed down the road, so I kept walking until someone pointed across the street to a clapboard shack just wide enough for one person to squat in. If I had known what awaited me behind that splintered door, I would have waited another five hours.

Toilets in the developing world treat you to more than just the usual "surprise." They can also be a learning experience. A "visit to the Queen" may require some planning or even flexibility. Often they require both skills, like when using the W.C. on a train in China.

To understand the context of this situation, you should know that the hard-sleeper car on a Chinese train has about ten compartments holding six beds each. That equals 60 people in each car...and two toilets. This means plenty of filth for you to endure in the W.C. And to avoid this filth requires planning. Thus I present to you:

Kolin's Six Virtuous Steps to Happy Hygiene

Step 1: Be Prepared.
Prepare for the battle against bacteria by grabbing your toilet paper roll from your backpack. (You *did* bring your own toilet paper, didn't you?!)

Step 2: Walk to the toilet.
Hide your huge, snuggly soft TP roll under your arm so that all the Chinese passengers don't gawk at the foreigner going to the loo. Walk with a confident step along the length of the car while looking straight ahead. Try not to make eye-contact with anyone; meeting a student who wants to practice his English at this moment would be extremely awkward.

Step 3: Open the toilet door.
You have reached your first obstacle: the door handle. You DON'T want to touch that thing. Just imagine all the unwashed, poopy hands that have closed that door behind them. Tear off two squares of paper to cover the palm of your hand as you grab the door handle. Stick the TP roll back under your arm. Open the door with your TP covered palm, then use your elbow to slam the door shut behind you. Use your protected hand to turn the lock, and then fling that diseased tissue to the floor.

Step 4: Locate the handhold.
Before you squat, you must search for the handhold. Remember—you are not on the smooth-flying shinkansen. This is a rocking and rolling second class Chinese train. You must be prepared for sudden jerks and jolts. Losing your balance and sprawling across the pee-slick floor would not be pleasant.

Screwed to the wall, about a foot above the hole in the floor is a metal handle. This is what you must hold on to to keep steady as you squat facing the wall. If you don't want to have nightmares, try not to think about the organisms crawling on this piece of metal. It has to be ten times worse than the door handle. So tear off two more pieces of toilet paper to protect your palm. You need to do this now because if you wait until you are squatting and *then* begin to tear off your paper, the train might jerk, you might lose your balance, and then you will be contaminated—either by falling on the floor or by steadying yourself with an unprotected hand on the wall handle. So get this paper ready before you pull your trousers down.

Step 5: Squat.

With the TP roll still under your arm, you have both hands free to pull down your trousers. Next, place both feet on the elevated footprints and squat over the hole while immediately grabbing hold of that handle with your protected palm.

Now, the art of squatting requires some flexibility. While riding the trains in China, my best friend Kevin would mutter the opening quote to this chapter as a squatter's prayer because Kevin always found the position of squatting painful to knee joints and thigh muscles. Ease of squatting is an acquired skill that most westerners have trouble mastering at first.

I have found that there are two basic ways to squat. First, there is the classic position that all Asians have mastered since they were toddlers. This is the posture where your butt cheeks touch your heels and each arm is extended straight out in front of you as a counterbalance. If you have traveled anywhere in Asia, you have probably noticed that this pose is not only useful for performing bodily functions in the W.C. It is also a restful pose for many

Asians, and you will see them on any street corner squatting while waiting for the bus, for example.

The second position is the less painful one which I call the "Ready, Set, Go" squat. Similar to a sprinter at the starting block, your left foot is placed flat on the floor slightly ahead of your right foot, with the left shin-bone almost vertical. Your right foot's toes are firmly planted in line with the left foot's heel and your right leg is bent below your body supporting most of your weight.

Step 6: Do your business and get out!

You don't want to linger in this W.C. The stink of 30 people's business explains the second part of the squatter's prayer above. After you have done your business, use some more toilet paper to protect your hand while you turn on the tap. If there is water, and if you are even luckier to find a sliver of soap, then wash your hands. If the water has run out, which often happens on a Chinese train holding a thousand passengers, then at least you know that if you have followed my instructions carefully, your hands will only be contaminated with your own bodily by-products. Repeat step three to exit the toilet, and walk confidently back to your bunk with toilet paper under arm.

Congratulations! You have beaten the bacteria on your first trip to the squatty potty. Of course, the instructions above don't only apply to the W.C on Chinese trains. Most of the above steps will be essential protocol for 90% of the developing world's toilets; so don't forget them!

A third skill you might need while visiting the toilet is adaptability. There are those times when your toilet paper runs out or there is no toilet at all. The first problem may seem more serious, but embarrassing situations may await the one who thinks he has found a private open-air W.C.

First, what can you do when you run out of toilet paper? If you are actually inside a toilet, the most obvious choice is to search for some paper towels near the sink. But what if there are no paper products to be found? My best friend Thomas has suggested using your socks, which indeed seem like a disposable part of a person's attire. If you have a spare t-shirt handy, this might also work. Tearing out pages from your science fiction novel can also serve as TP, and, depending on the type of paper, you might find these pages to be surprisingly absorbent. In this way, science fiction will finally serve a meaningful purpose.

But what if you are in nature and you run out of paper? The above-mentioned resources can be used, in addition to a variety of materials that Mother Nature has blessed us with. Leaves are the most obvious natural TP, though you must be sure of each leaf's innocuousness. I have heard that pine cones can be a bit pokey, but the swirling motion of cleaning oneself can be quite pleasurable for some people.

Once, in the *Tīan Shān* mountains while living with a Kazakh family (see Chapter Two), I ran out of toilet paper. All around were pine trees, and the open cones did not look inviting. I asked my Chinese friend Fred, who was with me, what I could use for toilet paper, and he said, "A stone."

"A stone?" I balked, "You must be joking." But Fred was serious. He told me to find a large smooth stone from beside the glacier-fed river that rushed past our shack and use that stone to wipe.

"The Kazakhs use them for toilet paper," Fred said matter-of-factly.

"How do you know that, Fred?"

"Because I saw their dirty stones thrown below a boulder on the side of the river."

OK. So I tried a stone. Though each stone could only be used at most twice, it indeed did a pretty good job of cleaning up.

While staying in Fred's village in Gansu Province in China, I ran out of toilet paper again. Fred's village was a cluster of five mud-brick homes in a forgotten corner of the Gobi Desert. The toilet was a hole dug in the sand near a corner of the exterior of his home's wall. Lyme was occasionally shoveled into the hole to prevent odor. There was no enclosure for privacy. To ensure your privacy, you simply announced to all in the house that you were going outside to the toilet. Then while you squatted in the open under the bright desert sun, you prayed that no neighbor would happen to walk by. This time, when I ran out of toilet paper, there were no trees or stones or water anywhere that could serve as a TP substitute.

"What can I do, Fred? I don't have any more toilet paper."

"Oh, that's no problem. There is plenty of toilet paper all around you. Just grab a handful of sand and rub up and down. It works really well."

"But isn't that a bit abrasive? You, know...rather scratchy?"

"Oh, no. Not if you make sure you pick up some fine sand. Not the sand that has big pieces or little stones."

"OK. I will give it a try."

Would you believe it? It didn't hurt at all. It was the equivalent of human cat litter clumping in your hand as you applied it to your rear end. What a wonderful innovation. Even more reassuring was the desert's never-ending supply of the stuff. My TP worries were blown away with the hot and dusty desert wind.

The second problem is hearing the call of Nature but there is no W.C to be found. In this case, you must search for your own toilet. Trees and bushes are likely candidates, but these hiding places aren't always as private as you may think. Even when you believe you have thoroughly surveyed the surrounding countryside for nearby people who might spy on you, in the developing world, someone can still suddenly appear as if from nowhere.

For example, in Ifrane, Morocco where I live, there are large expanses of evergreen oak and cedar forests. Natural toilets abound. But I am not the only person who frequents these forests; Berber shepherds also tend their flocks of sheep here, covering great distances in search of grazing in this parched Middle Atlas climate. Thus I have adapted the road-crossing mantra of **"Stop,**

Look and Listen" to decide whether it is safe to squat or not. Listening for people is just as important as the looking, especially when there are objects nearby behind which people may be lurking.

Yet even after applying these precautionary measures, I have still been surprised by a shepherd suddenly materializing from behind a tree. Since sheep are rather lacking in conversational skills, these lonely shepherds are always eager to chat with me. Unfortunately for them, I cannot speak Berber and they cannot speak French, and I am definitely not in the mood for niceties when Nature is calling.

Another magical appearing act happened on my trip to the Simien Highlands in Ethiopia. I asked our Land Cruiser driver to pull off to the side of the road so I could take a leak. I thought I had chosen a good location; the road we were on passed between open, empty fields of yellow stubble which extended at least several kilometers on either side. A 360 degree scan of the countryside assured me there was not a soul in sight. The nearest home was perhaps one or two kilometers away. Nevertheless, as soon as I unzipped my trousers, I heard the excited shouts of young female voices. I craned my neck to look over my shoulder as I continued to pee and was shocked to see three teenage girls about 600 feet (200 meters) away, sprinting toward me across a field.

"Oh, no!" I thought, "Where did they come from? Can't they tell from my body position that I'm taking a pee?"

I tried to hurry up, but the urine kept flowing as the oldest girl got closer and closer. I was almost done when this pretty young lady appeared at my shoulder. There was a split second of hesitation on her part as she suddenly realized what I was doing. Unabashed, she advanced a step or two to interact with me face to face. I embarrassedly swung away from her while zipping my pants, not quite having finished my business. If she had seen anything, I couldn't tell it from her expression. With the sweetest smile of perfect, gleaming teeth she said hello in English and held out some handmade jewelry, asking if I wanted to buy some. At that instant I was still overcoming my shock at her bold sales technique. She certainly had a captive audience in a urinating man, but my embarrassment compelled me to end our rendezvous as quickly as possible. I smiled at the girl, shook my head, then hopped into the Land Cruiser and closed the door.

These unexpected interactions are bound to happen eventually when traveling in the developing world. To keep them to a minimum, remember— **"Stop, Look and Listen."** Stop near your chosen open-air W.C. in a position where you have a good view of the surrounding countryside. Look for any people nearby who might be able to spy on you or who might wish to approach you for a conversation (or a closer look) at an inopportune moment. Listen for any sign of human activity nearby like the sound of voices carried on the wind, the chopping of wood, or the crunch of leaves under the feet of a sneaky shepherd. When you are fairly certain the coast is clear, you can get down to business.

Planning, flexibility, adaptability and a keen eye and ear for a safe, impromptu W.C. are all necessary survival skills for Nature calls in terra incognita. But there are times when no amount of planning or skill could prepare you for the horrific sensory surprises of a third-world toilet. At those times, you just have to grin and bear it...or, more appropriately, just bare it. That clapboard outhouse on the side of the road in steamy southwest China was one of those toilets.

Have you ever had the feeling, after holding it for a long time, that as you get closer to the john, the pressure inside you seems to increase exponentially and you can hardly keep it in? That is exactly how I felt after holding it for five hours in that wretched, sweat-drenched sleeper bus. That outhouse's splintered door, almost falling off its hinges, was beckoning me to fling it open and find release within.

A man exited the outhouse as I approached, and he held the door open for me. With my first hesitant step inside I penetrated a wall of oppressive, rank air as repugnant and clinging as a fart trapped in a wetsuit. This olfactory assault was compounded by an initial blackness so complete that I believed I had entered the metaphysical anus of the universe. As my eyes gradually adjusted to the shocking transition from glaring jungle sunlight to gloomy outhouse interior, I reluctantly let the door close behind me. There was no lock on the inside of the door, but no matter. An instinctual sense of foreboding compelled me to focus on the more important problem of finding out what I had gotten myself into.

My first thought was, "Where is the hole?" I wasn't going to take a single step further until I had identified the perimeter of the pit and where I should place my feet. I leaned forward and squinted at the black earth before me. My pupils were almost fully dilated now, so I could barely make out the borders of a square pit about three feet by three feet (one meter by one meter). Stretching across the gap, from the door to the back of the outhouse, were two planks of wood each about one inch (three centimeters) thick and each just wide enough for my foot. The planks were loose, so I tested the stability of each plank by gingerly placing my weight on them, one foot at a time, to make sure they wouldn't suddenly slide off an edge of the pit while I was squatting. Once satisfied that I wouldn't be sent swimming in a cesspool, I inched my way out over the abyss and assumed the position.

As I squatted, trying to breathe as little as possible, my eyes and ears began to fully perceive my surroundings. Flies buzzed incessantly in and out of the holes in the walls. They sounded especially numerous below my feet. I restrained myself from looking down, but in the corner of my eye, I couldn't help noticing some unusual movement below me. At first I thought it might be some perverted mammal like the coprophagous raccoons who like to grab a gooey snack inside the latrine boxes at Algonquin National Park in Ontario, Canada. Raccoons I could handle, but the thought of an unknown jungle critter possibly nipping at my most tender regions made me shiver despite the steaming stench of the cesspool below. I just had to see what was alive and moving down there.

Oddly enough, the movement wasn't isolated to just one spot. There was no scurrying of little feet in a corner. There were no quick furtive movements of some woodland creature. There were undulations—a constant and eerily silent rising and falling from one side of the pit to the other. The whole mass of stinking sewage seemed to be alive! I was horrified and confused: human waste does not move of its own accord. There was no sloshing or splashing to be heard because it wasn't the sludge itself that was in motion.

The wind blew in the trees outside allowing a ray of sunlight to filter through a crack in the outhouse wall. This slanting filament of light struck a portion of the filth below my feet, and then I saw what was alive. It was maggots. Tens of thousands of plump, glistening maggots writhing and seething over each other in endless waves as they feasted on the feces. They formed squirming mounds which floated on the cesspool's surface. In fact, it was impossible to even see the human waste since the maggots covered the pit so completely from one wall to the other. Pushing this nightmare from my mind, I finally attained relief. My contributions to their meal were soon engulfed by a swarming mass of hungry little bodies vying for a mouthful of the manna from above.

CHAPTER SIX

Shady Characters

"It is discouraging how many people are shocked by honesty and how few by deceit."
——*Noel Coward*

Claire was limping in agony while Saul called down curses upon the careless SUV driver. Claire, Saul and I had been walking across a parking lot in Guangzhou, China, chatting happily until Claire screamed out in pain. Saul and I were shocked and confused by Claire's sudden outcry until Claire yelled, "That idiot just ran over my foot!" A white Toyota 4Runner had been slowly approaching from behind and continued to advance, despite the fact that Claire was partly blocking the way through the parking lot. The Toyota's front right tire slowly rolled up and over Claire's left heel before she, with a surge of adrenaline, yanked her foot out.

"Stop!" Saul yelled at the driver.

As the Toyota slowed to a standstill, the front passenger rolled down his window. The driver leaned over his passenger to talk to Saul who stood at the window waiting for an apology. Instead, the driver professed innocence, blamed Claire for not looking where she was going, then began to drive away.

In a fuming rage, Saul kung-fu kicked the Toyota's door which proved quite effective in stopping the car. The driver slammed on his brakes, leapt out and confronted Saul, who was half his size.

"You're the one who obviously wasn't paying attention!" Saul shouted, "My wife's seriously injured! You will have to pay her hospital bill!" A shouting match ensued which Claire eagerly joined, giving the driver a piece of her mind.

By this time, as often happens in a country like China, a curious crowd materialized like vultures at a sky burial. Gawkers rubber-necked for a view of the action. These two dozen strangers jostled for position, squeezing me out of the scene. Though directly related to this drama, I was relegated to the rank of curious spectator as I hopelessly tried to press my way to the front of the crowd.

In the end, the driver fled the scene, not caring for Claire's plight, even if she was a foreigner. Saul memorized the Toyota's license plate, swearing that he would contact the police and have the driver brought to court. As the scene closed, the gossip-scavenging spectators dispersed on the breeze, while I stood there helplessly, offering words of comfort to both my friends and trying to cheer up the mood. After all, it was Valentine's Day. Once we got to our destination—a tasteful restaurant for our holiday meal—I offered to take a photo of the three of us.

I unzipped the outer compartment of my backpack to retrieve my camera and was flummoxed that it was gone! Where was my camera? I had even attached it to a very stubborn keychain clip so that it wouldn't fall out easily, but now my camera and the case it was in seemed to have magically disappeared.

Then it dawned on me what must have happened. Unnoticed among the hub-bub of shouting people and the pressing crowd, an opportunist had made his move. While I was busy trying to push my way to the front of the crowd, I was unaware of those brushing against me. While I was engrossed in the argument between Saul and the driver and concerned for Claire's well-being, I paid no attention to what was going on behind me. A petty thief, common in Guangzhou, took advantage of my distraction by deftly unzipping my bag to look for valuables. He found my treasured camera and even had enough time to zip up my backpack again before smoothly sneaking off with the goods.

I felt like a dolt. Even though Claire expressed her sympathy over my loss, I really couldn't complain. Claire deserved sympathy; the injury to her heel was much more serious than the pain I felt at having my camera stolen. Besides, I was partly to blame for my loss because of my inattentiveness. This hard lesson inspired my first rule in defense against shady characters:

Rule #1: Be alert and aware of your surroundings.

Being alert means taking the time to glance at the people around you. For example, is there an idle teenage boy nearby giving you the once over? Then move away. How close are people to your personal space? Is there someone close enough to look over your shoulder as you stand at the automatic bank machine? Then let that person use the machine first or find another ATM. In other words, a thief is much less likely to choose a person who is obviously on the lookout for trouble. But a plodding tourist, weaving like a drunkard with mouth agape while gazing starry-eyed at the Eiffel Tower is much more likely to be victimized.

Being aware of your surroundings means evaluating your environment for potential dangers. For instance, are you in a tightly packed mass of humanity, like on a subway, where you can't monitor all the people pushing past or brushing against you? Are you part of a crowd distracted by a street performance? Do you find yourself alone in a back alley or in a secluded corner of a park? In all of these situations, whether they occur during day or night, you are vulnerable to pickpockets or worse. Use your common sense; don't go down that alley and get back to a place where you are within sight of other people. If you can't avoid a crowded place, then keep your hands on your valuables with your back against a wall, if possible. Leaning against a wall will keep any wily hands from entering your backpack.

Once, in Funchal, Madeira, I was very aware that my surroundings had the potential for danger. My flight to mainland Portugal left early in the morning, so I roused myself before dawn to drive to the airport. Due to very limited parking in Funchal, I could only find a space 15 minutes by foot from my hotel. It was 4 a.m. on a Saturday morning, not long after the drunken carousing I had witnessed spilling out of pubs the night before. The narrow lane leading to my car was ill-lighted and derelict. Being accosted by a belligerent drunk was not how I wanted to end my holiday.

I was on the alert: To my right, a tall middle-aged prostitute lit up on a street corner. She wasn't going to cause me any trouble. A stout beer barrel of a man, dressed in slacks and a collared shirt plonked purposefully down the hill across the street from me. He was not a problem, either. Then a lanky man with sunken eyes and a disheveled look walked slowly behind Mr. Beer Barrel. Lanky Man took a look at me, did an about face, and began to follow me uphill on his side of the street.

This did not look or feel good. I picked up my pace while keeping note of Lanky Man's proximity with my peripheral vision. Then Lanky Man left my field of vision, and I heard him cross the street. Hopefully, I would reach my car, throw my bag in the trunk, get inside, lock my doors and pull away before Lanky Man came within range to do any harm.

I strode across the parking lot, and, when I reached my car, I glanced behind me to see if Lanky Man had entered the parking lot, too. He hadn't. Perhaps when I had turned right to enter the lot, Lanky Man had kept on walking up the hill. I relaxed as I opened the trunk and began to pack some clothes I had left there to dry. Just as I was closing the trunk, Lanky Man appeared in the corner of my eye about ten feet (three meters) away and closing fast.

Just before Lanky Man reached my left shoulder, I abruptly turned, glared straight into his bleary eyes and, in Portuguese, growled, "Que?"

This caught him by surprise, and he took a step back. I don't think he expected me to speak Portuguese since I looked like a tourist hiker with my big backpack. He made a furtive move to pass behind my back, so I turned to keep him face on.

"Tem um cigarro?" he muttered.

"Não!" I didn't have a cigarette.

We eyed each other for about three seconds until Lanky Man seemed to lose his resolve. He slinked away, and I watched him go until I saw him walk out of the exit at the other end of the parking lot and turn down the hill out of sight.

In this case, being aware that the time and place could be dangerous made me alert to the surrounding people. I identified a possible trouble-maker, tried to avoid a confrontation, then presented a strong, confident stance which, thankfully, made the shady character think twice. Of course, it helped that I am a man and that I was equal in size to my suspicious shadower. If I had been a woman in this situation, I would have thrown my pack and myself into my car, and I would have peeled out of the parking lot as fast as possible.

But sometimes, as with pickpockets, it doesn't matter whether you are a man or woman. If you aren't practicing Rule #2, then male and female are equal game. Can you guess what this rule is from the following stories?

STORY 1:

Downtown Mexico City. 11 p.m.

Just a few pedestrians wandered the sidewalks and the roads were empty. A stocky man in his early twenties made eye contact with me as we walked toward each other on opposite sides of the sidewalk. He quickly slid over to my side of the path to block my way and halted six inches (15 centimeters) away from my face.

"Can you help me, sir?" He asked in Spanish.

My right hand immediately grasped my camera strap as I quickly glanced to my left and right.

"Diga me," I asked him what he wanted as I turned sideways and took one big, slow step backward until I felt my backpack brush the wall of the building behind me. The young man stepped forward to close the distance between us.

"Do you have a light?" he smiled.

"No. Yo no fumo," I replied as I sidestepped along the wall trying to continue in my original direction while keeping an eye on the young man.

"Thanks anyway," the man waved as he turned and went on his way.

In Changchun, China, I often rode the rickety number 26 minibus from my school to ChongQing Lu, the busiest shopping street in town. The trip was usually uneventful: I rode to town, loaded my backpack to bursting with groceries, then caught the crowded bus home. But once every few months, after I got off the bus, I noticed something unusual; the outer compartment of my backpack was half unzipped.

"That's funny," I thought to myself, "I don't remember opening this." Then I would zip up my bag. The only item I ever kept in that compartment was my very practical roll of toilet paper, and that was still there, so I didn't give my unzipped backpack another thought.

Then one day, after finding my backpack half unzipped once again, I suddenly realized there might be a causal relationship between this very infrequent "memory lapse" and the bus I had just hopped off. My mind began to replay my bus ride. Where was I sitting? I was sitting on the right end of a low wooden bench with my back to the window and facing the other passengers. Where was my backpack during the ride? Since my backpack was empty, I left it on my back as I leaned against it and the window.

Then I remembered a clue. It was an odd feeling I had on the bus that the passengers were looking at me strangely. At first, I ignored the little voice in my head that told me something wasn't right because Chinese people usually stared at me anyway. But now that I thought about it more, I realized the three people opposite were looking at me in a nervous, guilty manner. Their eyes flitted from something near my left shoulder to my face and back again. Why did they appear nervous? What was happening next to me that warranted such worried expressions?

When I pondered their guilty glances, I recalled seeing that look on previous bus rides. Connecting this observation with my unzipped backpack led me to believe my fellow passengers' shameful faces were silent reactions to a crime in progress: On the bus, as I leaned forward with elbows resting on my knees, I exposed my backpack to the passenger on my left. Now that my bag was no longer pressed against the window, the pickpocket took his time to slowly unzip the outer compartment to inspect the contents.

Conducting this attempted robbery in broad daylight and in full view of three witnesses presented no obstacles. The thief counted on the egocentric, self-preserving Chinese custom of silent "uninvolvement" to protect him, and it worked. The witnesses had no way of knowing that all I stood to lose was a roll of toilet paper. Nevertheless, their inner battle of "alert the foreigner that he is being robbed" versus "shut up and keep yourself out of trouble" was clearly written on their anguished faces.

STORY 3:

The Barcelona subway train was about to arrive. I was wearing a waist pack with the zippered compartments at my back. As the train screeched to a halt, I thought it would be wise to slide my waist pack around to the front to avoid being pickpocket-ed when I merged with a throng of commuters. Just before I boarded the train, I verified that all my valuables were still there, then deliberately closed the zippers. But when I found a place to stand inside the carriage, I looked down at my waist pack and was astonished to see it unzipped! I wasn't disappointed because I didn't lose much. Only my leather Moroccan coin purse was stolen. The purse itself was worth about one dollar and it contained one Moroccan 50 centime coin. Fortunately, the thief's fleet fingers grabbed the first thing they found and left behind a much more valuable piece of paper—my 15 euro multi-day metro pass.

I was stunned at the speed and dexterity of this lift. In the three seconds it took me to climb the steps onto the train, I had been robbed, yet felt or saw nothing—even when my waist pack was directly in front of me.

You might have guessed by now that **Rule #2** is:

Guard your front and your back.

This means that when you are walking down a busy city sidewalk, take note of the people facing you, and be aware of how close the person behind you is. Scan the faces of those walking toward you while being constantly on the lookout for young men and children who make eye contact with you and who seem to be sizing you up. Be leery of these suspicious characters and move away from them if possible. Once they realize that you are aware of their presence, it is hard for them to approach you to make a hit. As for monitoring those behind, you could periodically glance over your shoulder, but that soon becomes tiring. Instead, use your ears to keep track of nearing footsteps. This takes practice, but eventually you will develop an instinctual sense of anyone entering your personal space from the rear.

A much easier way to guard your back is to never carry anything valuable behind you. Keep your handbag, camera and anything else of value in front. If your camera or handbag is on a strap, wear the strap over your head, not just your shoulder. Don't make the mistake I made in Story 3; just because your valuables are in front of you doesn't mean they are safe. Always keep one hand on your bag. Keep your bag's strap in a loose grip between thumb and index finger. A tight grip is easily broken by a thief's quick tug, but a loose grip will automatically tighten when it feels a robber's pull.

Practical safety tips like these are easy to follow, but sometimes a certain affective aptitude is necessary to keep you out of danger. My next rule is based on an intuitive ability to judge people and situations. For example, is that little voice inside your head telling you, "Something is not right here. Watch out!" or "I don't like the looks of this guy"? If so, don't ignore that little voice. Instead, you should practice:

Rule #3: Trust your instincts.

When I lived on Jeju Island in South Korea, I loved to ride my motorcycle to a "secret" entrance of Seongpanak Forest then spend the rest of the day wandering the secluded, silent wooded back roads. There was never anyone around, so I had the whole place to myself—except for one particular day.

On that day, I was surprised to hear the crunching of gravel under car tires getting nearer as I ambled along a road that flanked a burbling stream. Almost a whole year of forest exploration had passed, and I had never seen a car here. Notwithstanding, I glanced over my shoulder to spy an old Hyundai Sonata creeping around the corner. This purple, battered banger pulled up and kept pace with me as I walked. The driver, a pudgy 40-something Korean, rolled down his window, flashed a crooked smile, and asked me in stilted English where I was going.

"For a walk," I said without slowing. Hopefully this guy could take a hint from my short answers and unfriendly body language that I didn't want to chat.

"Where are you going?" he asked again.

"That way." I pointed straight ahead.

"You want come in car? I take you there."

Little cow bells tinkled an early warning in my head.

"No. I like to walk. Who are you?"

"I...I'm forest...uh...worker!"

Had the forgotten English word just popped into his mind or was this his impromptu identity? I looked at his clothes but noticed no uniform and no identifying emblem or badge on his shirt. I glanced at his dented, scratched car door but found no forestry organization's symbol emblazoned there. The little cow bells in my head morphed into a resounding fire alarm.

"I see. Have a nice day." I waved goodbye and picked up speed to indicate that, as far as I was concerned, this conversation was over.

The driver silently rolled up his window, his eyes fixed on me. Instead of driving away, he slowed down even further to drop in behind me, keeping his front bumper a steady six feet (two meters) or so from my heels. With the Hyundai on my tail, the next 10 minutes felt like hours as the fire alarm in my brain crescendoed into a blaring tornado siren. I started to sweat. My body wanted to run, but my mind told me to keep calm. I noticed that the sound of crunching gravel seemed to be fading. With the distance between me and my follower growing, I thought I might be able to make my escape. As I marched at a brisk speed-walker's pace (without the hip swaying), I began to devise a plan.

I was approaching an extensive grove of saplings planted just off the road and protected by a gate six-foot (two-meter) high wire fence. On a previous walk, I found that I was skinny enough to fit between the loosely chained halves of the gate. If I walked across this grove, I could squeeze through the opposite gate and emerge at the far west side of the forest. It was a shortcut that bypassed circuitous logging roads, saving me about an hour's walk to one of my favorite viewpoints on the southeastern flank of Halla Mountain. If I could get to that grove and through the gate without Mr. Fake Forest Worker seeing me, then I could escape my stalker.

Until now, I had been determined not to look nervously over my shoulder and reveal the fear on my face to the shady driver, but after turning a sharp bend in the road, I couldn't resist a peek. When I saw that the false ranger wasn't immediately behind me, I took off running. The gap in the forest that marked the entrance to the fenced saplings was in sight, and the car still hadn't turned the corner. I dove behind some bushes near the gated grove, crouched as low as possible, and peeked through the branches while praying that the Hyundai would drive on by. Once the impostor's purple mobile crawled past, I bolted for my shortcut.

As I threw my backpack over the fence and squeezed through the gate with a rush of adrenaline, my heightened hearing detected the skid of tires and the whine of the Hyundai reversing. The driver knew I had turned off the road when he couldn't see me anywhere on the long, straight stretch ahead of him. But he was too late. I was sprinting through the grove, already more than halfway across and thankfully on the far side of a hummock that blocked the driver's view of the opposite gate.

I made it to my favorite viewpoint unseen, and spent the rest of a balmy spring day sitting in my camping chair reading a book and occasionally surveying the forest-covered oreum below me. I kept an ear out for passing cars and heard the crunch of gravel at the viewpoint's trailhead several times, but no one came walking through the forest toward me. I returned to my "secret" entrance without event, and my motorcycle, thankfully, was still as I left it. I never saw the fake ranger again.

The ranger seemed friendly enough in the beginning, but the evidence contradicting his supposed identity was more than enough to make my little inner voice shout, "Get away from this man!" The situation I just described might be so obviously suspicious to you that the proper response of running away seems to be more common sense than intuition. But you'd be surprised how many naively trusting people there are in this world. Without them, scammers would be out of business. And that is why I made this final rule:

Rule #4: Beware of overly friendly people.

As a lone traveler, it is always refreshing to meet friendly folk. It restores my faith in the goodness of humanity when I meet a personable stranger who is willing to help with directions or to recommend a local restaurant selling hearty, good-value meals.

But then there are those who have made an art out of being friendly, and their act is very believable. These are the scammers and con artists—in general, very shady people.

At Stazione Centrale, the main railway station in Milan, there are some decent looking young ladies, cleanly dressed with smiles on their faces, who stand beside the metro ticket machines. They are there to help you. Or so it seems. This was one time when I failed to follow Rule #3; I didn't listen to my instincts.

When I saw these girls, my initial thought was, "Wait a minute...Why is there a girl standing next to every ticket machine? And why are there no passengers buying tickets from those machines?" But then I thought, "What could go wrong? All I have to do is put my coins in the machine, press the right buttons for the ticket I want, and collect my ticket when it falls into the tray at the bottom."

My assumption was wrong in just one point. I walked up to the machine and the girl asked me in Italian what kind of ticket I wanted. She quickly realized I didn't speak Italian and switched to English.

"Hello, I help you? What ticket you want?"

"A day pass," I told her.

I watched her deftly flip through the English menu and press the correct button on the screen for a day pass. The machine displayed the amount that I had to insert—4.5 euros. The girl held out her hand for the money, I gave her the change ("Oops!" I thought), and she briskly inserted all the coins in the slot as I watched the machine subtract each piece from the 4.5 euro total. I saw the ticket drop into the tray, but before I could reach it, the girl's hand reached in and, in a flash, she presented me my ticket before my eyes. My instincts told me something wasn't right, so I inspected my ticket. It said, "Single Journey—1.5 Euros."

"One euro for help," the girl brazenly held out her hand expecting a tip for her "help."

"You're not getting a euro!" I half-shouted at her. "You already got three euros from me." I looked her in the eye, sneering at her gall. At the same time, I was annoyed with myself because I fell for this scam when my instinct had warned me before I even approached the machine. I couldn't be bothered to argue with her over three euros. There were no police around, besides, what good could they have done? She would have protested innocence and would have pointed at the ticket in my hand that supposedly proved she had helped me. She had tricked me fair and square, but how did she do it?

For the next few minutes, I puzzled over what had gone wrong. I ran and re-ran the scene through my mind, incessantly analyzing each step of the ticket-buying process to imagine at what point she had cheated me. I concluded that in one swift move she had picked up my 4.5 euro ticket with her left hand and presented me a previously-bought 1.5 euro ticket with her right hand. I didn't notice my purchase slipping into her pocket as I ogled the cheaper ticket she distractingly held two inches (five centimeters) from my face. I should have listened to my instinct. I should not have trusted this overly eager young lady so intent on "helping" me.

Not an hour had gone by before a man from sub-Saharan Africa approached me in front of Milan's famous Duomo, the largest cathedral in Italy. He was selling worthless tourist knick-knacks to make a living.

"Hey, my friend!" he sauntered over in a feigned jovial mood. "What's up?" He held out his fist for a fist bump.

Did I have "sucker" written all over my face? I ignored his extended fist, turned away, and continued reviewing my recent shots of the Duomo in my camera's viewfinder.

The young man gave up on the fist bump and gently laid three loosely-twined strings—which, I think, was supposed to be a bracelet—on my shoulder.

"For you, my friend! It is free!"

"Take it," I growled.

"No problem, man! It is free!"

"Take it!" I put his string on the step beside me. "Nothing is free." I knew that accepting his "free" gift would be followed by a demanding sales pitch to buy one of his more expensive items.

He gave me a sour look and cursed me in his language as he grabbed his string and stalked away in search of a more naïve tourist.

Both the girl at the ticket machine and this young man had their simple set routines. They milked their successful scams over and over with unsuspecting tourists. But there are more elaborate "friendly" scams than this. I fell for one of these con jobs in Casablanca, Morocco. This scheme demanded opportunistic creativity and some very convincing story-telling.

He looked like a weather-worn sailor, and that is why I believed him. He was also older—probably in his mid-sixties—and that made me trust him even more. I met this hefty, muscular mariner outside the mediocre Chinese restaurant where I had just eaten supper. It was about 11 p.m. and there were very few people out and about. He was loping heavily along on his way to somewhere when I stepped out of the restaurant and onto the street. In the corner of my eye, I noticed this man with his grizzled beard angle his course toward me until we were walking side by side.

"Hello, sir. Where are you from?" he asked in English.

Being wary of strangers at this late hour, I eyed his dirty blue jeans, stained beige sweater and ill-fitting red wool hat, trying to judge his character. His eyes were squinty but had an earnest gaze, and his rotund, fuzzy belly, peeking from below his sweater, lent a playful jollity to his demeanor.

"I'm Brazilian," I finally answered after deciding it would be alright to chat with this man while I walked.

"Ah! I have been to Brazil!" he exclaimed happily.

"Really? Where have you been?"

Here was a test to see if this guy was genuine or not, I thought.

"I'm a sailor. I have been to many ports in Brazil."

"Like where?" I challenged. He might know Rio or São Paulo, but no others.

"Oh...Salvador, Fortaleza, Santos, Niteroi..."

I was impressed! This man knew his Brazilian geography. I was almost thoroughly convinced that he was genuine. His English was quite good, too, which seemed to support his persona of a well-traveled man.

"Can you do me a favor?"

"Here comes the catch," I thought.

"What favor?"

"Can you change some dirhams and give me some dollars?" he asked.

Ah! Here was the scam I'd been waiting for. I knew there was something up this sailor's sleeve. My salary was in dirhams, so I could answer the man honestly.

"I don't have any dollars. I live in Morocco," I explained.

"Then can you change some dollars into dirhams for me? I have a big bill that I need to change before I go on the ship tomorrow morning."

This sailor wasn't going to give up easily. But this seemed like a reasonable request, and since I knew the proper exchange rate by heart, I knew I could give him the correct amount of dirhams without being swindled.

"OK, so where is the money?" I asked.

"Oh, I don't have it here. It is at my home. Come to my home, and I will give you the money."

I wasn't about to be lured to this man's home in the middle of the night. He was twice my size and could easily overpower me. No, I was going to keep walking toward my hotel and stay out in the open in sight of the few pedestrians around me.

"No. You go to your house and bring me the bill. I will wait here in this café for you." In the back of my mind I wondered why

I was helping this stranger anyway. It was late and I wanted to get back to my hotel to sleep. "I have to stop being so nice and accommodating!" I mentally castigated myself.

"Not this café. I know a better one over there," he motioned with his hand to a busy establishment just before us.

Being surrounded by people would be a good thing. I would certainly feel safer in there than out here on the desolate, lampless street.

"OK," I agreed.

He led me by the elbow into the café and down the long central aisle past several tables until we reached a booth.

"Ah! Mustafa! Salam wu aleikum!" the sailor greeted a friend who just happened to be alone in a red velvet booth big enough for six. Mustafa was a wiry fellow with a sharp chin, aquiline nose and the piercing gaze of a hungry eagle. He flashed a flawless, gleaming smile as he extended his hand to greet me.

I sat opposite the sailor and Mustafa (I never knew the sailor's name), and we agreed to have a chat over a pot of sickly sweet mint tea before the sailor went to get his money. The sailor did most of the talking. It seemed that Mustafa's English was very limited. The sailor regaled me with tales of his world travels while Mustafa just stared at me, a knowing smile curling the corners of his lips.

Once the tea was finished I volunteered to pay. Unfortunately, the smallest note I had was a 200 dirham bill, and I knew the tea would only cost around 30. The sailor volunteered to take my money to the cash register with such alacrity that I became suspicious.

"Well, the cash register is at the back of the restaurant, and not the front," I thought, "So that means that I can watch him pay for the tea from where I'm sitting, and he can't make a quick dash out the door with my change. Even if he does try to walk past without giving me my change, I will just stand up and block his way." That was wishful thinking.

Leaving with my change was exactly what the sailor had in mind. After paying for the tea, he wheeled around and bulldozed through waiters and clients on his way to the front door. I jumped up to stand in his way, and Mustafa tried to grab the sleeve of my shirt to pull me back down but lost his grip. The sailor, stone-faced, glared at me, then brushed me aside like a limp spinach leaf with one sweep of his Popeye arm.

I rushed after the sailor and tried to hold him back by grabbing his arm, but he shook me off like a freshly picked booger as he headed out the front door and into the street. I was shouting, "Hey, give me my change!" while Mustafa followed, cursing me in English with a sudden and astonishing fluency. So Mustafa could speak English after all...

Out on the sidewalk, the sailor continued his brisk march, but I hounded his heels like a pestering, yippy Pomeranian. When my efforts to pull him to a halt failed once again, I jogged past the sailor, then turned to face him. I stopped his progress by placing my right hand on his chest and pushing with all my strength against his stubborn momentum.

"Give me my 170 dirhams!" I demanded.

Mustafa got right in my face and feverishly howled a stream of exquisite maledictions. The sailor side-stepped to the right, and so did I. He feinted left, and I stayed with him. After a few seconds of fox-trotting, the sailor, disgusted with my mosquito-like whining, swatted me against the wall of a building and headed for a black alley.

Our tangling trio delved deeper into the Stygian recesses of ever-thickening darkness. In the time it took me to recover from being smashed into a wall, the sailor and Mustafa had gained a considerable lead. Now their murky forms were blending with the Cimmerian blackness. I began jogging to catch up, but then I stopped.

What was I doing? Had I lost my mind? Why should I follow two men who were bigger and stronger than me down an inky, forsaken alley and possibly risk my neck for a measly 170 dirhams (about 20 U.S dollars)? I laughed out loud at my preposterous persistence, especially when I thought of the 1800 dirhams I still held safely inside my jacket pocket. If the sailor had been inclined to violence, he could have torn my cash from me like a fox plucks feathers from a chicken. Mustafa and the sailor knew nothing of the riches they could have gained.

When Mustafa heard my laugh echo around him, he looked back at me with fear furrowing his brow. My derisive chuckle was incongruous to this scene, and that unsettled him. Mustafa pushed on the sailor's back to propel him forward, and I smiled as I watched them melt into the engulfing gloom.

CHAPTER SEVEN

No Lines in the East

"Observation: Standing in line is a
form of oppression."
— John Green, The Fault in Our
Stars

The soldier's baton cracked mercilessly upon their shoulders, pummeling them into submission. Men cringed and cried out in pain as the wooden lightning flashed against any offender who was out of line.

"This is how things should be," I thought to myself as I reveled in this scene of unmitigated justice. Finally, something had been done to control the masses.

Before you accuse me of vicarious sadism, allow me to explain: The end of Chinese New Year had come, and millions of people— university students and migrant workers mostly—had descended upon every railway station like Genghis Khan's rabid hordes. This heaving, pushing, shoving, crying, desperate mass of humanity— the world's largest human migration—gathers every year across

China. This mayhem coincided with the end of my winter holiday. This meant that I usually had to fight disorderly mobs of travelers to get my ticket back to Changchun Teacher's College.

But not this time. To my pleasant surprise, each ticket window at the Chengdu Railway Station was guarded by two teenaged soldiers—one beating anyone who dared weasel their way to the ticket window by squeezing in from either side of the queue, and another soldier keeping people in single file where the metal banisters leading to the ticket window began. This was a definite improvement. Without the prospect of wrestling my way to the front of the line, I immediately relaxed. In a culture where queuing is a foreign concept, this enforced order was like a refreshing dawn mist rolling over the Namib's dunes.

I had been living in a desert of disorder where no green shoot of decorum could sprout. I had survived four years of battling to board buses, of elbowing to enter eateries, of shoving to secure a seat on every form of motorized transportation. Buying stamps at the post office, purchasing any kind of ticket, and being served in a supermarket always involved some degree of looking out for number one. Finally, "first come, first served" had gained a tenuous foothold in the concrete of the Chengdu Railway Station.

Queuing is a western idea. In general, there are no lines in the east. In countries like China, where one must compete for attention against millions of other small fry, the squeaky wheel gets the oil. In everyday reality, this means the loudest shouter and the most persistent pusher will be attended to first. The more "in your face" you are the better—no matter how annoying this might feel to your western sensibilities. If you enter a bus station and perceive a free-for-all at the ticket counter, then plunge right into the *mêlée*. But don't dive in unprepared. You'll first need to learn **"Kolin's Devious Tricks for Self-Promotion."**

Trick #1: Go directly to the front of the line.

What are you doing standing helplessly at the back of that unruly mob? If you don't give up your western sense of protocol, you'll be there all day! Do you see anyone else hanging around with their hands in their pockets hoping the ticket seller will notice them standing civilly in line? No. Do you really think the supermarket clerk will be nice enough to say, "Oh, look at this foreigner who is waiting so patiently to be served. You've been waiting for quite some time, haven't you? How can I help you?" Come on! No one will know you exist unless you make yourself known. To get heard fast, you must go directly to the front of the line.

The front of the line may be hard to distinguish when the shoving crowd constantly shifts shape like an amoeba. Within this organism, the pushing people displace each other as they fight to get near the nucleus of attention. Every so often, someone is ejected like pus from a distended pimple, only to push their way back in through the cell wall of tangled arms and legs. Ignore those squabbling organelles and head straight for the nucleus—the ticket seller or supermarket clerk.

But don't push your way forward from the back. The trick is to walk calmly to the front, then sidle in from the right or left. To do this you will need to use some force.

Trick #2: Use your elbows.

God gave you elbows, so use them. They aren't just for arm bending. Those pointy protrusions are great pokers, too. Now don't think that I'm promoting assault and battery. I don't want you to start bashing teeth or smashing sternums. A slow but firm pressure in the belly will do.

Once you are near the front, face forwards and squeeze your body sideways into any gap you can find. Once you have one shoulder and arm wedged against someone, start pushing back with your elbow, gradually increasing the pressure so that the person behind you moves just enough to create another space into which your body can slide—hopefully in a forward direction.

Imagine that you are swimming with your elbows. The bodies around you are the waters you must push aside and behind to propel you forward. Ideally, each elbow jab will be in the stomach of the person before you, thus pushing each new wave of human flesh backward until you reach the shore. In other words, this process is a series of squeezes and jabs; wedge half your body before the person in front, then elbow back, and repeat.

"But I'm not strong enough to elbow big men backward," you might whine to yourself.

Never fear. There is an easy solution. All you need to do is use the people around you for leverage. You won't need much effort to push with your elbow if you follow these steps:

Step 1:
Raise your hand to shoulder height with palm forward. Then use your legs to push your raised arm between two people.

Step 2:
Place your palm flat on the upper back of the person in front of you. Then jab your elbow as high as you can into the belly or chest of the person behind you so that your forearm is firmly wedged between the person in front and the person behind.

Step 3:
To make a gap into which your body can slide, incrementally lower your palm and then raise your elbow, repeating the movements until your forearm is horizontal or until there is enough space into which you can slide your body.

Step 4:

Slide your body sideways as far as possible into the space between your palm and elbow.

Step 5:

Drop your elbow. You will now be pressed between two bodies, but a little further into the crowd than before. Look for another person to wedge yourself in front of and repeat Steps 1-5.

If you still think you are too small or too frail to push back the masses, then please read on.

Trick #3: Small can be good.

Are you a petite lady or a vertically challenged man? No need to worry. You can use your diminutive stature to your advantage in this situation.

When you think about how people squeeze together in a crowd, you will realize that it is usually one torso pressed against another. But below the waist, there are plenty of spaces around the legs and feet. If you want to buy that train ticket, you should swallow your pride, duck down low, and search out those spaces that larger people can't fit into. You might occasionally find yourself in unlikely places, but your quick forward progress by weaving through legs and around bellies will make the discomfort all worthwhile. Victory will soon be yours when you pop your head up at the ticket counter to the surprise of the ponderous, pot-bellied fellow behind you.

Trick #4: Hold your place in line.

Just because you are now face to face with the ticket seller doesn't mean the battle is over. You still need to fight against others using the same devious tricks you just employed. Until your transaction is complete, you must prevent anyone else from cutting in front of you.

Once you are at the front, the biggest threats will come from your left and right. You're not the only person who knows about Trick #1—sneaking a lateral attack. That is why you must immediately block anyone from squeezing in, under or around you. To do this you need to hold on. Hold on to anything, and hold on with both hands. Hook your fingers into the metal grate at each side of the ticket window. Grasp the counter top firmly or latch onto any metal railings. Lean back into the pressing crowd and brace one foot against a wall if necessary. Wearing a large backpack can come in handy since it makes you twice as wide. Use this extra girth to fill dangerous gaps. You can even swing your backpack into the face of a lateral attacker to effectively stymie his advance. This may seem rude, but remember—western ideas of politeness and personal space don't exist in this situation. It is every man for himself, and you must use all means possible to win your prize.

Trick #5: Shout loudly and wave your money.

Now that you are secure in your pole position, you will need to get the ticket seller's attention. Oh. Did you think that you were the only one at the head of the queue? Well, that is another western concept that you will have to do away with. For example, if the counter in front of the ticket window is a meter long, that means three other Chinese people can be jammed in that space with you. This is why strong vocal chords and a fistful of cash are necessary.

To get the ticket seller's attention, you must shout your demand as loudly as possible:

"One hard sleeper to Beijing on the 25th!"

Shout this request over and over while waving your money in the ticket seller's face. If you can, jam your hand through that little opening in the window. When the ticket seller looks you in the eye and asks you what you want, you know you are close to your goal.

I said, "close to your goal" because what you want may not be available. Be sure you have several backup requests that you are ready to shout out or else you will be pushed out of line. Then you will have to repeat the whole line-cutting process, and you don't want to go through that again.

Your interaction with the ticket seller might go something like this:

"What do you want?" (Customer service is another western concept your Chinese ticket seller has never heard of.)

"One hard sleeper to Beijing on the 25th!" you scream over the background noise of the mob behind you.

"Mēi yǒu," says the ticket seller. You will soon come to hate these two words meaning "not have."

"What about on the 26th?"

"Mēi yǒu."

"The 27th?"

"Mēi yǒu."

"Do you have a soft sleeper for the 25th?"

"Mēi yǒu."

"A soft sleeper for the 26th?"

"358 yuan."

Bingo! You have found a berth to Beijing at the busiest time of the year. You'd better count out your money as quickly as possible and shove it through the window before the crowd gets impatient and ejects you. The ticket seller passes you your ticket, and you verify that all the details are correct. You walk away quite pleased with yourself. You have successfully squelched your western mores to win attention and claim your prize.

When you see the impossible crowds cramming into the train on the 26th, you realize that your new-found skills of self-promotion will come in handy more often than you thought. You won't need a baton-wielding soldier to get you safely to the front of the line. You now have your own effective crowd-beating weapons—a quiver full of Kolin's Devious Tricks.

CHAPTER EIGHT

"That's not what I meant!"

*"If you talk to a man in a language
he understands, that goes to his
head. If you talk to him in his own
language, that goes to his heart."*
—Nelson Mandela

"學而時習之 不亦說乎"
(Xué ér shí xí zhī, bù yì yuè hū.)
*"Is it not enjoyable to learn and
practice what you learn?*
—Confucius

*"Consuetudo certissima est
loquendi magistra."*
*"Usage is the best language
teacher."*
—Marcus Fabius Quintilianus

L earning a new language can be frustrating, but it can also be fun. I have learned Portuguese, Spanish, French and Chinese to varying conversational levels and always with mistakes in grammar and pronunciation. Mistakes are an inevitable part of language learning, and if you are afraid to make mistakes, you will never learn.

I have told several of my shy students, "You just have to open your mouth and say it." Don't worry about making a mistake. When babies are learning a language, do we consider them as stupid because they make mistakes? No. In fact, we find their mistakes endearing, and we never fault them for it. I have found the same to be true when I'm the "baby" learning to speak a new language. Most people appreciate my efforts to communicate in their own language, and those who really care help me to improve my speaking by politely correcting my mistakes. That is the most productive way for me to learn a language—by making a mistake and then correcting it. So when you are in a new country trying to pick up some phrases in the local language, remember:

Language Learning Lesson 1: Open your mouth and speak, even if you make mistakes.

The fastest way to learn any language is by immersion. Living in Changchun, China forced me to pick up the phrases necessary for everyday life. Living in China wasn't like living in South Korea. In South Korea, I lived for one year without hardly ever saying a word in Korean to anyone. If I did speak Korean, it was only the two phrases I ever learned—"*Anyanghaseyo.*" (hello) and "*Kansamnida.*" (thank you). In South Korea, I could shop for my food in a gigantic supermarket, and at the cash register I only had to look at the digital display to know how much to pay. When I went to a restaurant, I always chose one which had an English menu or where photos of the available dishes were displayed prominently on the wall. All I had to do was point to the food I wanted. But in China there was no way for me to avoid verbal interaction if I wanted to do anything.

For example, I couldn't cook well (still can't), so I sometimes went to a restaurant by myself. Since there was no translator to help me, I first had to memorize the names of some dishes I liked which I had eaten with my friends Claire and Saul. Just making the waitress understand which dish I wanted was a small success in itself. Then I had to master sentences like, "Please give me chopsticks, tea, napkins, the bill."

Similarly, when buying vegetables at the Balipu market, I had to memorize all the names of the vegetables – potato is *tŭdòu*, tomato is *shìzi*, cucumber is *huānggūa*. Next it was necessary to learn sentences like, "I want one *jīn* (catty)." "That's too much." "Enough!" and "How much does it cost?" Of course, knowing all my numbers was crucial in order to pay the right amount, and my listening skills had to be fine-tuned to hear the price correctly.

Traveling in China also forced me to practice my spoken Chinese, such as when buying train and bus tickets, asking for directions, or booking a room in a hotel. Understanding the response to my questions depended on nonverbal cues from facial expressions and body language in addition to much intelligent guessing about what several crucial words might mean. After every journey in China, I returned to my home in Changchun with a larger Chinese vocabulary and improved listening skills.

Intelligent guessing was a key skill when I went to my favorite restaurant. The owner, Sun xiao xi, who later became a good friend, would always come and sit across from me and begin chatting. I really just wanted to have a quiet meal alone or read a novel while I ate, but to be polite I listened and tried to guess what she was saying. It didn't matter to her that I knew almost no Chinese at all. She used her simplest vocabulary aided with many gestures and facial expressions to get her general message across. To help out, she would even throw in a few Japanese words that she knew came from English (Sun xiao xi could speak Japanese fluently). She never gave up. She was persistent, and now I'm thankful for that because through her persistence she taught me much Chinese. By the end of my second year in China, I could have a simple conversation with her for up to two hours. Each time we talked, I learned a few new words.

Changchun's taxi drivers were also a catalyst for my Chinese language skills. The first time I stepped into a taxi I was inundated with questions I couldn't understand. All I could do was shrug my shoulders, smile and say, "*Tīng bù dǒng,*" literally, "I don't understand what I hear." This was frustrating for both the inquisitive taxi driver and for me. I *wanted* to understand. So during every subsequent taxi ride I listened carefully to the driver's questions and tried to memorize the nonsensical syllables. When I returned home I would repeat the questions to a student and get the English translation. Next, I would ask the student to translate my English response to each question, then I memorized my answers in Chinese. Thus, the next time I entered a taxi and heard a familiar question, I could give an answer to satisfy the driver's curiosity. After a while, when a taxi driver asked me: "Where to?" "What country are you from?" "How old are you?" "Are you married?" "How much money do you make each month?" "What's your salary?" "Do you like living in China?" "Do you like Chinese food?" "Do you like Chinese girls?" "Why don't you find a Chinese wife?" "Do you miss your family?" "How many people in your family?" "Do you like Brazil or China better?" "Do you have cold weather like this in your country?" "Aren't you cold?" I could answer all their questions!

Being able to speak with the locals made life in China so much easier and more pleasurable. So if you want to have a more positive experience traveling or living in a new country, then remember:

Language Learning Lesson 2: Speaking the local language, even if it is just a few phrases, will endear yourself to the locals and make your stay easier and more enjoyable.

In no way was my Chinese perfect. The four tones of Chinese were a constant problem at first. If you are unfamiliar with the Chinese language, you should know that each word uses either the first (‾ , a high tone), the second (/ , a rising tone like the intonation at the end of a question in English), the third (˅ , a falling and rising tone), or the fourth tone (\ , a falling tone; a short sound like shouting "ya!" when doing a karate chop). If you don't use the correct tone for a word, it won't have the intended meaning. Let me give you an example from one of my own mistakes.

Sometimes when I went to a restaurant I would ask for a cup of tea. The word for cup is *bēizi*. For almost a year I continued to ask for what I thought was a cup of tea. Only later did I learn that what I had been saying was *bèizi* which meant quilt. For so long I had been asking for a quilt of tea and none of the waitresses had said a word about it! Once I was eating at a restaurant with a few students and there weren't enough chopsticks. When I went to ask for some from the waiter, he happened to ask if everyone had a cup. I substituted a similar word and said, "Yes, we all have *bízi*" which meant we all had noses!

Other times, when I heard an unfamiliar word or read a new word in *pīnyīn*, the romanization for Chinese, I would fall back on my limited vocabulary. I often mistook the new word for one I already knew that had the same or a similar pronunciation but with a different tone.

For example, after class one day, my students were competing in a long-distance relay race against other university departments. Near the end of the relay, Henry put the English department in fourth place, closing a wide gap between himself and the third place runner. Then Jackson passed the third and second place runners to put us in the lead. Little Tracy (she was just about five feet/150 cm tall) was the last runner, and could she ever run fast! Her tiny legs were a blurred windmill!

While Tracy ran her laps, her classmates Cheer and Republic were cheering, shouting what I thought was, "*Jiāng yŏu! Jiāng yŏu!*" ("Soy sauce! Soy sauce!") I thought, "What on earth are they saying? Is this Tracy's nickname?" I asked Alice what Tracy's Chinese name was, and it was something totally different from what I was hearing the girls shout. When I got home I asked my teaching colleague Claire, and she explained that they were actually shouting, "*Jìa yŏu!*" which means "Add oil!" In other words, "Go faster!" since you have to add "oil" (gasoline) to go faster. I suppose it would be something like saying, "Step on the gas!"

On the flip side, I encountered in China a plethora of humorous English mistakes or odd uses for the language. Without a doubt, using English is extremely popular in China. The following are a few examples of how the Chinese have used English to sell a product.

English words abound on young people's clothing. For example, I saw a college-age student wearing a jacket on which was written, where the name brand would be, "Sun and Water together make Perfect." I saw boys wearing blue sweatshirts that had "GIRL GIRL GIRL" printed all around the bottom. Conversely, the girls all bought the pink version of the same sweatshirt with "BOY BOY BOY" at the bottom. I had a student who wore a vest with the letters "BO" printed over her heart. My favorite was a fake Chicago Bulls jacket with a genuine-looking copy of the bull's face on the back. Above the bull it said "CHICAGO" and below it read "HEAD COW."

Product names can also be amusing. During my friend Kevin's first week in Changchun he was really feeling homesick and depressed. One morning when he awoke, he looked at the headboard of his bed to read this well-wishing name brand: "HappyPleaseBestSmile." It cheered Kevin right up. I always smiled when I saw "Instant KLIM" ("MILK" spelled backwards) at the supermarket. I couldn't help laughing when my taxi drove past the "LAME FURNITURE" store. My favorite was a brand of cigarettes called "Victom"!

On some food products, if you turn to the back of the package, you will find a scientific description in English meant to extol the product's health benefits. The attempt to sell me is a grand one, but it would be so much more effective if only I could understand the English. Below is an example quoted from a powdered milk package (mistakes uncorrected):

INTRUDUCTION

Zinc is one of principal trace element that human body contains, so it is called "flower of living."

Metabolic relationship between Zn and human body is very close, and be paid more attention by persons on nutriology. This product is developed for current situation, which the rate of lacking Zn is very high, directed against population in our country, especially those people in the area that regard grain as staple food or polished food.

This product take fresh Zinc milk, high-quality white granulated sugar as material adopt prescription of Beijing Nuturtion Source Research Institute, strengthen sorts of vitamin and Zn, Fe reasonably and made with science method. And it is noted for good quick dissolved, rich nutrition, and strong sweet smelling of milk.

Sometimes at a restaurant your chopsticks come in a plastic package along with a moist towelette. On the reverse of one such package it said, "RISING TOWEL DISINFECTED MANY TIMES AND THEN SUPERFINE MADE, CAN DISINFET QUICKLY, IT ISN'T POISONOUS OR HARMFUL. ITS SMELL IS BETTER." Just how do you make something "SUPERFINE" I wonder? I guess I would have to visit the Superfine Factory myself and see how those superfine men and women operate the superfine machinery that made my Rising Towel superfine. I was glad that my Rising Towel could "DISINFET QUICKLY", but isn't it a given that a moist towel you receive with your meal won't be poisonous? I guess some people just take this fact for granted, so the Rising Towel Company wanted to remind us just how good we have it! It also sounds nice that "ITS SMELL IS BETTER," but better than what?

I have also kept a packaged moist towelette that I received when flying with China Northern Airlines. The boast made about this napkin was rather alarming in what it implied: "This product can thoroughly kill virus of hepatitis, Venereal disease and lymphocyte in one minutes kill staphy lococci bacterium coli, tubercle bacili and fungus in two minutes." The airline food was bad enough, but to think that fungus, bacteria and the viruses of hepatitis and venereal disease might be lurking nearby or could even be on my hands was enough to make me lose my appetite altogether!

During one summer holiday in Qinghai Province I bought some dried yak beef. The yak meat had an unusual curry flavor so I wanted to see why. Turning the bag over I read: "Burden (meaning "Ingredients"): The best yak beef, refined salt, refined sugar, chilli powder, chinese prickly ash, curry power, perfume and so on." I wondered what the "and so on" consisted of, and no wonder the yak meat tasted so much like curry with all that "power" in it! Then there was more helpful information: "Store up the way: lay in the place of the dry ventilating and cleening." It also said, "The edible way: After it is opened, you can have it at once." I was quite thankful for these instructions. I'm not so sure I could have found the edible way on my own.

Greeting cards and signs were not immune to errors. My student Alaska received a card from a friend that said, "Babe a Monberful Day!" A popular greeting card wish was, "Wish you

Happy Every Day!" Some signs I saw in public were rather enigmatic such as a warning sign that simply read, "Please, pay attention to." Pay attention to what?! One sign at Hanasi Lake in Xinjiang read, "Please don't litter the rubbish." The Great Wall at Simatai is a rugged climb on the other side of a river. There is a bridge, but one sign advertised, "Climb the Great Wall by boat." My favorite is a sign in Dalian to keep people from walking on a gorgeous lawn. It said, "NOBODY DOESNOT LOVE THE GREEN LAUN."

Above all, my students at Changchun Teacher's College provided me with the greatest amusement. To begin with, some of the English names they gave themselves were unique, if not puzzling. Most girls like cute names that are short, easy to say, and end with the letter "y". In one class I had students named Milly, Tilly, Lilly, Holly, and Polly. There was always a Nancy or a Shirley in every class. Yet there were girls like Enigma, Eternity, and Nirvana who just had to be different. Normal names for boys are Frank, Nathan, Derrick and Kerry. Then there were exceptions like Beatles who liked the rock group. Eleven got his name because he was the eleventh boy to arrive at his dormitory when he was a freshman. Second chose his name because according to the English saying, "Every second counts." One of my student friends wanted to be the "Best" in middle school. Somehow this name morphed into the moniker by which everyone now calls him – Pest. Fortunately, he doesn't live up to his name.

Jeff and Bonney, my good friends who were also teachers in Changchun, told me they had one student who named himself Panasonic because he liked electronics. Another boy at their school called himself Afrank. Not simply Frank, but *Afrank*. None of us could figure out why the student added the "A" to Frank, and perhaps the student didn't know himself. Hearing his name made me think of a frankfurter or a wiener. I thought it would be so much more amusing if he changed his name to Awiener. Then I could chuckle inwardly each time he introduced himself to other foreigners saying, "Hi, I'm Awiener," and catch their reaction.

Kevin once told me why his student Marlboro chose his name. Marlboro told Kevin, "Because of the first four letters. To me they mean 'Men Always Remember Love!'" Which made me wonder, "Boys Only Remember (?)". Another time a student asked Kevin, "Can I be Christ? My previous foreign teacher said that I couldn't be called Christ. Will you let me be Christ?" Kevin replied, "No, but you can be Chris if you like."

Conversations with my students also provided some humorous English. For example, I smiled to hear Phoebe say that the opposite of doing something discretely was to do it "cretely." It certainly sounded logical. My student Daisy, who came to visit me weekly, was a never-ending source of funny mistakes. She made a mistake similar to Phoebe when I asked Daisy if she knew why a beeper has its name.

"Yes!" she replied confidently, "Because a bee is an insect and it makes a sound 'BZZZ'..."

"No, Daisy. A beeper makes the sound 'BEEP'," I explained, "And even if the first part of the word 'beeper' was 'bee', then what's a 'per'?"

Daisy and I had supper together one night. After we ate, I was washing the dishes and poured some leftover tomato soup down the drain. The inside of the drain was black with rotting food material from previous meals, and some tomatoes got stuck in the drain. As I picked out the pieces by hand, I said to Daisy, "Look! Soup a la mold!"

Daisy said, "Huh?"

So I asked, "Do you know 'mold'?" Daisy didn't know what mold was so I explained it. "And 'a la'" I continued, "means 'with something'. As in 'apple pie a la mode.' That means apple pie with..."

Daisy burst in shouting, "I know! Apple pie with mold!" Perhaps my explanation wasn't clear enough for her.

Once, Daisy and I went to downtown Changchun to visit the Cultural Square. At the square we flew a kite and took some photos together. After developing the photos, Daisy looked at one of a large bronze man that stands in the square's center with his arms outstretched toward the sky.

"What's the word for this man made of metal or a person made of stone?"

"Statue," I pronounced authoritatively.

"What?" Daisy asked meekly.

"Statue!" I said louder and with more force. Daisy appeared shocked.

She blinked once or twice, and then with a questioning, almost hurt look said, "Why? Stat me? Stat me?...Stat you? I don't understand!"

Poor Daisy thought I was damning her with a new curse—"Stat you!"

Another mistake happened during a role-play in oral English class. First, you must know that in Chinese, to ask a yes or no question you add the particle "ma" at the end of the sentence. So, in this particular role-play a student fell in love with the teacher. When Hazel, who played the teacher, discovered her student's affections she said in amazement, "He loves me ma? He loves me ma?" It was amusing to me, but for the students it was hilarious when someone used "Chinglish" (Chinese mixed with English) like this in the classroom.

Some students, like Nancy from Grade 98, like to create their own new words. Nancy told me that when English movies are translated into Chinese, the language sounds ugly. She called it "chubbish" meaning that the Chinese sounded like rubbish. Another example was when I told Judith, Pest's girlfriend, about a man I heard of who had long leg hair like myself. This man allowed some of his female friends to braid all of his leg hair. Judith was amazed and exclaimed, "Wow! His leg hair was just like a sonic!" Since Judith didn't know the word "hedgehog" she assumed the character "Sonic" from a Nintendo video game was the proper word for that animal.

I had a student named Claire, also from Grade 98, who is now my good friend. When I had a cold once, Claire took me to the school clinic to get some medicine. I asked Claire to please read the back of the box and tell me in English what the medicine would do for me. She read for a few minutes then said rather casually, "Oh. It says here that it will kill your virtue."

"But Claire," I laughed, "I want to keep my virtue! My virtue is a good thing! I don't want to kill my virtue!"

At first she looked confused, then suddenly realized, amid a burst of giggles, that she really meant "virus."

Students who come from the south of China often seem to have the most difficulty with English pronunciation because of the influence of their local Chinese dialect. Many have trouble with the sounds of the letters "l" and "n" and "v" and "w". Not only is their English affected, but also their pronunciation of *pǔtónghùa*, or Mandarin Chinese, which is the national standard dialect belonging to the northeast. Below is an example of how a local Guangdong (Cantonese) dialect completely altered a Chinese-to-English translation in my Oral English class.

Helen, of Grade 95, was such a sweet little girl with a tiny, gentle voice. During one Oral English lesson she became quite sentimental when describing to me the fond memories of her girlhood in her village. Her bucolic hamlet, located just outside of Shaoguan in Guangdong Province, is too small to be on the map. Behind her home were some hills where every day she would take the family's water buffalo to graze. She really enjoyed the quiet times on the hills and would stay there all day looking after the water buffalo. When she mentioned that she took her lunch with her to the hills, I asked her what she ate for lunch.

She said, "Lots of delicious food. What I liked best was –" Here she turned to her friend Theresa sitting next to her and asked, "How do you say (Chinese word) in English?"

Without hesitation Theresa replied, "Hoofs."

So Helen turned to me and said, "Yeah, I really liked to eat hoofs."

"Hoofs?!" I exclaimed, incredulous, "You ate hoofs?"

Helen said yes.

"Hoofs," I said, "are the feet of cows and horses." Helen turned to Theresa to verify the word.

"Yes, hoofs!" she said with conviction.

I looked at her for a few seconds, still not believing that this dainty little girl had enough power in her jaws to chomp on the giant toenails of a cow. Then I said, "OK...Please, continue," since I didn't want to hurt her feelings by telling her I thought her favorite food was revolting.

Helen continued her story happily, but I wasn't listening. I was still trying to imagine pretty Helen gnawing on her hoof lunch. When she finished I moved on to listen to other students. Not five minutes later I heard gales of laughter erupting from Helen and Theresa at the front of the classroom.

"Come here, Kolin! Come here!" Helen called with streams rolling down her cheeks.

When I got to the front of the class, Theresa was laughing so hard she lay across her desk in spasms of laughter, unable to speak.

"Not hoofs! Not hoofs!" Helen shouted, her hand waving frantically in the air, "Not hoofs, Kolin! I mean water chestnuts!"

The problem was that since her classmate Theresa was from Changchun, where people speak standard Chinese, she misunderstood Helen's dialect word for water chestnuts as being similar to the *pŭtónghùa* for hoof. I was quite glad that Helen didn't really eat hoofs, though I never fully believed it, suspecting some error. Later I actually went to Helen's village near the hills and ate "hoofs" with her for lunch.

Karen, in Grade 94, was a southerner from Guizhou Province. (In light of my previous story about the phrase "Add oil!" it is interesting to note that Karen's Chinese name is Jiang yao and her nickname actually is *jiang yǒu—soy* sauce!) Karen was quite proud of her province and once showed me a brochure about Guizhou. She pointed to pictures of Huangguoshu (Yellow Fruit Tree) Falls, the largest waterfall in China. There were also photos of the Miao minority people. Karen kept repeating that this was a eunuch minority in China. For a while I was thoroughly confused. If this was a eunuch tribe, then how could it continue its existence? Finally I figured out that she meant the Miao were a *unique* minority, not a eunuch one! I used a dictionary to show her what she had said, and we had a good laugh about her mistake.

Almost all my Chinese students, like Karen, could laugh at themselves for their errors in English. Some were embarrassed, yes, but they could take the teasing of their classmates and myself in good humor. I'm pleased my students could laugh freely in my classes. I'm even happier they felt comfortable enough to take small risks by speaking out.

The lesson for you, the traveler, is that when you are learning a new language you will make mistakes. Don't be so hard on yourself. You need some humility. Some people take themselves too seriously to laugh at their language mistakes. I'm glad my students and I weren't that way because even though we made many errors, we learned from them, and we still had fun.

CHAPTER NINE

To Speak or Not To Speak

*"Remember not only to say the
right thing in the right place, but
far more difficult still, to leave
unsaid the wrong thing at the
tempting moment."*
—*Benjamin Franklin*

S o you're feeling linguistically superior because now you can
speak conversational Chinese (or whatever the language
might be). Not bad. Congratulations. But what you might not
realize is that when you are in the land of your newly acquired
tongue, there is a time to speak and a time not to speak the
language, especially when you find yourself in trouble with some
power-wielding figure in a uniform. I know what you're thinking:
"But I won't get into any trouble with the police. I'm not a

criminal. I don't plan on breaking any laws." Well, neither did I. Yet several times this meek, skinny, bald-headed, bespectacled English teacher has quite unintentionally found himself racking his brains for the right answer in order to escape the stern glare of some overbearing authority figures.

To facilitate your future escape from legal entanglement, I have developed two maxims that will help you, as a foreigner, decide when to speak or not to speak the local language:

Rule #1: If you have purposefully been a little naughty or if you are obviously guilty, even though you broke a rule unwittingly, then don't speak the language.

Let me give you an example of when I failed to follow this rule.

To get to the Trade Mansion and other shops in Changchun, China I usually took the bus. With my university in the countryside, the bus was the most convenient option, especially in the subzero winter. The distance to Chongqing Road, the main shopping district, really wasn't that far, so in good weather I would ride my bike there, usually arriving more quickly than any bus because I didn't have to stop for passengers and could ride through traffic jams. That is what I had done on a warm spring day in 1996.

Upon arriving outside the Trade Mansion, I locked my flashy mountain bike to a green metal fence that divided the sidewalk from the road. Usually, people lock their bicycles in a designated parking area where hundreds of bikes are lined up neatly as close together as possible and are overseen by the bicycle parking lot attendant. After you have done your shopping, you pay the parking lot attendant the five *mao* due him, unlock your bike, then squeeze your way down the cramped aisles between the rows of bicycles. I chose not to do this because it was more convenient to park my bike opposite the Trade Mansion's front entrance. This way I had a shorter distance to walk into the store, and after shopping I could easily get to my bike and ride home.

I always carried a sturdy three-foot (one-meter) long bicycle lock with me in addition to a clamp lock installed on my front wheel. I passed my bicycle lock through my frame, back wheel and around two fence posts, then headed off to shop.

Bike theft is rampant in China. You would have thought that everyone had a bicycle of their own already, so where is the demand for a stolen bike? But apparently grand theft cycle is big business, and there is always someone who wants to save some *yuan* by buying a hot bike. My very first bike in China, a Flying Pigeon (a good brand) was stolen from right outside my apartment. Someone told me that my bicycle would be safe if I just locked the front wheel and left it in the stairwell outside my front door. To my chagrin, I awoke one morning to find that my Flying Pigeon had flown.

In fact, later I heard that it is a known and brazen scam for one or two men in a truck to cruise apartment complexes picking up bikes from stairwells and nonchalantly placing them in the back of their vehicle. If someone asks why they are removing a bike, they just answer, "Oh, I'm picking up this bicycle to fix it. The owner isn't home, so he said I could stop by to collect the bicycle." Very few people would have the courage to get involved by saying, "Hey, I've never seen you around here before. And why is that bike's front tire still locked?" Now you can understand why it was a reasonable concern that my bike might get stolen a second time.

Instead, when I emerged from the cold concrete halls of the Trade Mansion into the warmly glowing sun, I was shocked to discover that my bike had not been stolen but rather it had been made positively un-stealable! A six-foot (two-meter), rubber-coated, heavy-duty chain with links as long as my thumb had been wrapped around my bicycle twice like a golden boa constrictor, held together by a portly lock worthy of Fort Knox. I looked around in bewilderment, trying to fathom who would do such a nonsensical thing to my bicycle. Stealing my bicycle I could understand, but who on Earth would want to make my bicycle safer? I gazed at the lock and then looked around several times, wondering if anyone was going to show up to remove my lock. If no one came, then how would I ever find them? How long would I have to stand there waiting for this mystery person to appear?

After what seemed like a long time (probably just four or five minutes), two policemen in their 20's showed up. The cop in charge (there often seems to be a boss and a lackey in pairs like this) started jabbering away in Chinese to no effect on me. I had not a clue of what he was saying. Couldn't he see that I was a foreigner who spoke very little Chinese if any at all? After a withering harangue, he paused as if expecting an answer.

It was at this point that I broke Rule #1. I was guilty of something, though I didn't know what, and I made the mistake of speaking to him. "*Tīng bù dǒng*," I replied, saying that I didn't understand.

His next sentence I did understand. He shouted in Chinese at me, "You do understand! You said '*Tīng bù dǒng*'! You can understand me!" He seemed very angry. Oh dear.

The policeman then made a key gesture that turned on a light bulb of understanding in my mind. Suddenly everything was clear. With an all-encompassing upward sweep of his hand, he brought my attention to a giant sign, perhaps six feet (two meters) tall and nine feet (three meters) long, looming right above my locked bicycle. On the sign was an extremely long numbered list of sentences to which the cop pointed while shouting, "Number 24 says blah, blah, blah and number 37 says blah, blah, blah." Finally, I understood that all of those numbered items were rules and that I had apparently broken one or two of them by locking my bicycle to the fence rather than securing it in a parking lot.

My problem was that I couldn't read Chinese. So I made the mistake of saying, "*Kàn bù dǒng*," letting the policeman know that I couldn't read—literally "I can't understand what I see."

"You can understand! You said, '*Kān bù dǒng*'! You can understand what it says here! Number 24 says..."

"Here we go again," I thought. We went around in circles for several minutes. I repeated "*Kān bù dǒng! Tīng bù dǒng!*" with ever increasing volume and persistence and the policeman countered by insisting that I understood because I could speak two phrases in Chinese.

Until now, Mr. Silent Cop had just stood there watching this comedy. Suddenly, as if having an epiphany, he gave a stiff elbow jab to his mate's ribs and exclaimed, "Hey! He's a foreigner!"

Silence. Mr. Loud Cop stared at me in shock, as if scales had fallen from his eyes and he was seeing me for the first time. I stood there thinking, "Duh! How could I be Chinese with my big foreigner's nose and all this hair on my arms and legs?" How could they not have noticed this sooner?"

"Are you a foreigner?" the first cop asked, still incredulous.

"Yes. I'm a foreigner," I stated as matter-of-factly as I could, trying not to sound condescending.

"Ah! *Dùibuqǐ! Dùibuqǐ!*" Mr. Loud Cop apologized profusely as he immediately opened the lock and unwound his chain from my bicycle. Both policemen grinned and waved affably as I rode off into the choking traffic toward home.

All of this would have been resolved instantly if only I had followed Rule #1. If I had stood there dumbly or had said but one phrase in English—"I don't understand"—then I could have been on my way 15 minutes sooner.

An altogether different police encounter happened in 2008, during my three month tour of Mexico. This incident with the military police was of a much more serious nature. Thankfully, I obeyed Rule #2.

Rule #2: If you are innocent, or if you strongly believe that you are, then speak the language.

I had just arrived by bus in Patzcuaro from the town of Morelia. I looked rather travel weary in a grubby t-shirt, and I couldn't wait to wash my greasy face. I hefted my black military-sized duffel bag onto my shoulder and limped across the road to a hotel listed in my guidebook. No one was at the reception, so I lumbered down the front steps into the street.

"*Señor*! *Señor*!" I heard someone yelling behind me.

I turned to see a machine-gun toting, body armor-wearing military policeman waving at me to follow him.

Since I'm not one to argue with weapon-bearing men, I immediately and silently followed him, wondering, "Now what?" I knew I was innocent. I was fresh of the bus! I hadn't been in Patzcuaro for more than five minutes. I couldn't possibly have broken any rules in that short a span.

So I heaved my burdensome bag along behind this man until we reached a pickup truck marked "Policia Militar" on the door. Two armed men sat in the back, and two more were in the cab. The men in the back smiled faintly and nodded their heads in greeting. The policeman who had picked me up told me to put my bag in the back of the truck and to open it up.

"No bombs in here are there? Ha, ha, ha," one cop in the back half-joked in Spanish.

Immediately I realized that I had just been picked up under suspicion of terrorism! I couldn't say that I blamed them, really. I certainly fit the physical profile: shaved head, brown skin, wiry frame, sporting a half-grown prickly beard and carrying a suspiciously large black duffel bag.

Knowing my innocence, I followed Rule #2 and answered in Spanish, "No. Just some clothes," and I showed him.

"Get in the front please."

One policeman slid out of the cab for me to get in next to the driver, and then swung himself back inside, effectively wedging me between them like linguiça in a bun. This was comfy. Then the driver asked me for my identification.

At this point, I realized I had better think fast. I had several options. I could give him my U.S driver's license which might not be "official" enough. I was traveling on my Brazilian passport which might possibly give me some favor in the eyes of the police. After all, everyone loves Brazilians—the creators of samba and the perfecters of football. But I didn't want to hand over my passport for fear that the police might confiscate it; then I would never be able to leave Mexico for Dominica to visit my sister Kirstyn. Finally, I decided to give the driver my U.S Resident Alien card. If they really suspected me to be a bomber, surely my U.S origin would allay their suspicions. Besides, if they kept my green card it was replaceable and not necessary to my future travel plans.

I gave the driver my green card believing that my I.D would remain in the same vehicle with me. To my disappointment, the driver gave my green card to the cop who picked me up. This cop then hopped in another police vehicle and disappeared into traffic.

"Uh....Where is he going with my card?" I asked in Spanish, afraid to hear the answer.

"Oh, don't worry," assured the driver, "He's going to the police station where we are going, too."

"I certainly hope so," I thought.

We drove leisurely through the traffic and chatted along the way. Oh, the conversation seemed casual enough, but the questions posed sounded more like interrogation than small talk.

"So what are you doing in Mexico?"

"Traveling."

"For how long have you been in Mexico?"

"Five weeks."

"Where were you before Patzcuaro?"

"Morelia."

"And how long have you been in Patzcuaro?"

"Just five minutes. When that policeman called me, I had just gotten off the bus."

We arrived at the police station and parked outside the front door. No one got out. We all just sat there. I was sandwiched in a cop bun with the two behind guarding my bag.

"What are we going to do now?" I asked.

"We're waiting," came the terse reply.

So we waited. I supposed we were waiting for the policeman with my green card to check out my identity.

To my relief, after about ten minutes of silence, the policeman who picked me up emerged from the station with my I.D in hand.

"Here's your I.D," he said smiling, as he handed me my green card. "Have a nice day."

The cop next to me started to open the door and get out of the truck so that I could leave.

"Um...wait a minute," I said to the driver. "When you found me, I was looking for a hotel in the town center. Now we're far from there, and I don't want to walk all the way back. Would you please take me back to the center so I can find a hotel?"

"Sure! No problem." All the way back, my two cab mates told me about the best hotels that were clean and cheap. They even dropped me off right at the door of a recommended inn. I waved goodbye, thankful that I had my I.D back and that my calmness and answers in Spanish had allayed their suspicions.

Only later in my holiday did I hear of the 2008 Morelia grenade attacks. The attacks took place on September 15 during the Mexican Independence Day celebration when thousands of people gathered in Plaza Melchor Ocampo, the main square of Morelia. Two grenades, thrown into the crowds, killed eight people and injured more than 100. The first blast occurred around 11 p.m. on the Plaza as Governor Leonel Godoy led the *grito*, the traditional *vivas* to the heroes of the nation. The second grenade exploded a few minutes later in an alley four blocks away. The police accused the drug cartels for the attacks, specifically La Familia Michoacana. La Familia Michoacana denied it, blaming Los Zetas, another drug gang. A week later, just around the time that I arrived from

Morelia in Patzcuaro, the military police arrested three men of Los Zetas as suspects for the attacks.

I knew I was innocent when the Mexican police picked me up, but sometimes the situation might not be so clear cut. Sometimes Rules 1 and 2 might need to be bent according to the circumstances, the personality of the authority figure, and the level of your innocence. "How can you have levels of innocence?" you might ask. My illegal entry into Hungary was just such a time when my culpability was not so black and white.

◆◆◆

At the end of that day, I could hardly lift the spoon to my mouth. Though my face was almost in my cereal, I could barely muster the strength to feed myself. My legs were lead, and my stomach was cramped as tight as Mr. Smithey's buns. All I could get down me was a bland bowl of cornflakes, though I knew I was starving after not eating for 10 hours. I had never been so thoroughly exhausted before.

After teaching a routine day at Jana Amosa Komenskeho High School, I decided that I still had enough time to go for a bike ride. I got home at 5 p.m. and had three more hours of daylight to enjoy. In Slovakia, if it didn't rain, it was a good day for a bike ride, and a sunny day was a rare event of which to take advantage.

For a year and a half, my second-hand blue ten-speed was my ticket to sanity. After a mediocre day of teaching, when students would misbehave and apathy hung in the air like a wet blanket, I would jump on my bike after school and zoom off into the pristine countryside, not knowing where I was going and not worrying about time. I just went, and with that motion the day's troubles would soothingly melt away like butter in the sun. This was one of those days.

I headed south out of Košice, where I lived. I rarely took this route because I knew that south of the city the Hungarian plains began. Fields for miles is all I would see. I preferred the forested hills to the north of Košice with their winding country roads meandering up through glossy trees and down past jubilant meadows. But this time I went south just for a change.

As I pedaled, the idea struck me that I would ride to Hungary. I knew the border was only 14 miles (22 kilometers) from the edge of town, so why not, since I was already heading in that direction. I didn't know which road to take, but that didn't matter. I was on a main road that was heading directly south (I had looked at it before on a map of Košice), so I just trusted this road to take me to the border.

After an hour of riding, my trust seemed a bit misplaced because the main highway narrowed into a two-lane country road that became a cobbled street in the village of Seña. This village street petered out in a resplendent field of rape flowers. For a moment I was puzzled. The best thing to do right then was to sit down, enjoy the view and drink some water.

Seña. The name sounded familiar. Where had I heard the name of this village before? Ah yes! I remembered that Reverend Mikuláš lived in Seña. He was a Lutheran minister who also taught at my high school. But it was no time for a visit. I had a self-appointed mission to reach Hungary or bust. As I looked around I noticed that across the field, in the distance, a car drove south on a road I hadn't noticed before. I must have missed a turn. So I straddled my bike, retraced my pedaling, followed my nose and soon was on my way to the border.

My sense of direction was rewarded after half an hour when, up ahead, I could see several rows of trucks and cars lined up at what appeared to be a border crossing.

"Yes, it's a border crossing," I thought, "...or is it?"

Vehicles were waiting to pass through several narrow lanes between kiosks. It looked like a small-town version of the U.S-Canada border. But where were the guards? There wasn't a border patrolman in sight! There were none in the kiosks and none walking around. There was no one to stop these cars and trucks from driving right on through. Yet all of the motorists just sat at their steering wheels with eyes glazed over. A few truck drivers looked me up and down with expressions of sheer boredom.

It must have been coffee break time for the police or whoever it was who was supposed to be in the kiosks. I just couldn't understand how all of them could go on break at once without leaving even one person in charge or on watch. I was confused. Could this really be a border crossing with such lax discipline, with such a laid-back work ethic? With these doubts in mind, I decided there was only one way to find out if Hungary really was on the other side, but I wasn't about to wait in line with all the other vehicles.

I formulated a plan. Off to my left I noticed a lane that branched from the main road I was on. This lane dipped down a small hill and appeared to go around an office building next to the row of kiosks. "Let's just see where this goes," I thought to myself. "If a guard sees me and stops me, then I'll just turn back. But if no one sees me, I'll continue pedaling until I reach the other side. Then I can see if I'm in Hungary or not by looking for a sign that says 'Welcome to Hungary,' just like they always have a welcome sign when you cross a border into a country. If there's a welcome sign, then I'll know this really is a border crossing." The thought crossed my mind that I should have a passport with me, but I easily squelched that inconsequential worry for the sake of the adventure.

I began to ride very slowly, very casually down the lane. I kept my eye out for a guard, but pedaled as naturally as possible. "Just look confident, like you know where you're going," I thought to myself. Before I knew it I was around the office building and on the other side. No one had seen me or stopped me. The only person paying me any attention was a bored truck driver who seemed a little surprised to see me appear from nowhere. I pedaled across the line of kiosks, in full view of any guards who might have been watching, to approach a large rectangular sign standing in the grass at the roadside.

The sign said, "*Magyar Köztársaság.*" I couldn't believe my eyes! I really was in Hungary. I had just crossed an international boundary unchecked and unnoticed by any policeman, and I didn't even have a passport! By this time it was 7:30 p.m. and the sun was setting, so I decided to take a picture of myself in front of the sign and get out of there before anyone noticed. As quickly as possible, I set my camera on its tripod and balanced the tripod on my bike seat. I was worried that my camera's flash would attract too much attention, but I wasn't about to miss this opportunity. I had come too far to forfeit this photo which would serve as a souvenir and proof of my adventure.

I took the photo, and as I put my camera back in its case, the knot in my stomach that had just begun to form suddenly tightened when I saw a Hungarian guard walking out of the office toward the first truck in line. The guard stood next to a truck only 30 feet (10 meters) away. How was I going to get back across the road, down that lane and around the office building to Slovak safety without being noticed? I decided to wait until the guard's back was to me. While the guard was busy talking to the truck driver, I slowly, casually, and as silently as possible began to pedal my bike across the road toward the lane. I had almost reached the lane and was nearly out of sight when the guard suddenly turned around with a look of shock and disbelief on his face. I was slightly annoyed that the truck driver who saw me must have tipped off the guard, but that thought only lasted a second. The guard yelled, "Hey!" (or the Hungarian equivalent) and I took off, pumping my legs like pistons powered by adrenaline.

From the sound of the guard's clacking shoes beating the pavement behind me, I was aware that he had not chased me around the office building but had cut through the kiosks, trying to catch me on the other side. But he couldn't catch me. I looked behind me and saw that, in the ten seconds it took me to reach

PUSHED FROM A TRAIN

Slovakia, I had put 300 feet (100 meters) between myself and the exhausted guard, and the distance was growing. In the waning twilight, all I could distinguish was a lanky, red-haired man flailing his arms and ranting in incomprehensible Hungarian. It occurred to me that he could jump in a police car and chase me down, but I just kept on pedaling for my life.

"POP!!" At the sound, my heart jumped into my throat. When I looked behind me, my heart sank to my stomach. My back tire had suddenly gone flat. It was no use pedaling now, and the guard knew it. He walked up to me, fuming, as I dejectedly turned my bike around and walked it toward him. I was caught. The guard barked in rapid-fire Hungarian, but he could see that I understood nothing. Rule #1 began to work in my favor. I knew I was guilty, but my ignorance of Hungarian was frustrating the guard to no end. He grabbed my arm and motioned that he would put handcuffs on my wrists and take me to jail.

I could just picture the Košice paper's headline the next morning: "Jana Amosa Komenskeho High School's foreign teacher caught after crossing Hungarian border illegally; Lutheran Reverend Mikuláš called to post bail." I would be a disgrace to my students, my school and my colleagues. But it would make a good story to tell the family back home.

Since the Hungarian guard couldn't communicate with me, he handed me over to a calmer, kinder looking Slovak authority. Maybe I still had a chance of not going to jail.

"*Passport?*" he asked me.

"No passport," I told him in English, still following Rule #1.

"*Identifikácie?*" he asked with raised eyebrows.

I showed him my Slovak ID from Košice. He said something that I guessed was, "Why are you crossing a border with no passport? Are you crazy?!" I did understand the word "auto" as he waved at all the cars in line.

At this point I decided to speak Slovak. Even though I knew I was guilty, I decided to use the ambiguity of the empty kiosks in my defense. After all, it really was confusing, wasn't it? I feigned my innocence.

"*Áno. Auto, autobus. Bicykel, neviem.*" I shrugged my shoulders trying to tell him in my baby Slovak that yes, I saw the cars and buses but I "didn't know" that bicycles couldn't cross the border.

"*Päť minút. Do Maďarsko, foto*, then *Slovenska Republica.*" I told him I had only gone to Hungary for five minutes to take a photo and then had come right back to Slovakia again. The guard looked at me slyly as he inspected my ID card.

"*Takže ste učiteľ angličtiny, nie? Žiješ v Košiciach, áno?*"

I nodded yes, that I was an English teacher living in Košice. The guard handed me back my card then waved his hand as if to get rid of me. My heart leapt for joy when I understood that he meant, "Go back to Košice!"

But my troubles were not over. Now I had to ride 14 miles (22 kilometers) home on a flat tire! Before I set off, I carefully scanned the road where my tire had popped, but I found no glass, no sharp stones, and no shards of metal. I inspected my tire, but nothing was stuck in it. There was no gash in the rubber.

God must have popped my inner tube. That was it. God wanted to teach me a lesson not to break the law. He must have reached down with his fingernail and punctured my tube to stop me from escaping that Hungarian guard. In addition, I had committed a cyclist's cardinal sin—I had brought no spare tube or tools. Now I had to pay the penalty not by going to jail, but by riding home for 14 miles (22 kilometers) on a flat tire.

By now it was 8 p.m. and it was already dark. In the Slovak countryside, traffic is almost non-existent during the day, let alone at night. At this hour, I wasn't likely to hitch a ride with anyone. I thought of stopping in Seña again to ask Reverend Mikuláš to give me a ride home, but I was too sheepish to bother him. It was my fault that I was stuck out there, and I was determined to pay my penance by getting myself home. So I set off in my lowest gear, dragging my flapping tire behind me.

The dense darkness engulfed my lonely frame. After an hour my legs began to cramp, and I had a stitch in my side. It was now 9 p.m. and I hadn't eaten anything since lunch eight hours ago. I was running low on energy and forced my legs to pump at their strained yet steady pace. To make matters worse I was riding into a 15 mph (25 kph) wind. Riding on my flat began to feel like I was pulling 30 pounds (15 kilos) of road kill.

"At least it's a warm night and 22 kilometers isn't really that far," I tried to console myself, "It could be worse. At least it isn't raining."

Then the heavens let loose with a drenching downpour that soaked me through. My cotton t-shirt clung to me coldly like soggy saran wrap. Suddenly, 22 kilometers seemed like an eternal bike ride across the Gobi Desert.

By the time I got to Main Street Košice, my legs no longer obeyed my brain's command to pedal. They dangled limply from my saddle like sausage on a meat hook. I was only five minutes from home, but felt like a drained battery. To propel myself the final distance, I swung my legs back and forth, pushing forward scooter-style.

It was 11 p.m. when I slurped that last spoonful of soggy cornflakes. I groaned at the thought of dragging myself out of bed at 6 a.m. to teach the next day. Then I thankfully realized that teaching tomorrow was better by far than cowering in a Hungarian jail cell unsure of my fate. Choosing the right time to speak and knowing when to be silent won me the sweet luxury of sleeping in my own bed that night. Despite my cramped legs, starving stomach, and popped tire, I had to admit that the chase, my capture and the photo of my international visit were all worth it. I couldn't wait to tell my friends and family the story of my illegal bike ride to Hungary.

Claire was truly my savior. She helped me so much during my first
year of adjusting to life in China. Here we are on a trip in the
countryside near the China-Russia border, 1995.

Ever since we circumnavigated China together in 1995, Kevin and I
have gone on an adventure almost every year. In 2017 we visited
the Black Hills, South Dakota, U.S.A just before I had the pleasure
of being a groomsman at his wedding.

The first class I ever taught—Grade '93 English Department students at Changchun Teacher's College, China. I'm in the front row, fourth from left. 1996.

My wonderful students are the reason I have remained a teacher for 22 years. This pose was my students' idea for our end-of-semester class photo in Jeju National University, South Korea, 2010.

"That's not what I meant!": Funny signs in China—PAY
ATTENTION TO....KOLIN!

"NOBODY DOESNOT LOVE THE GREEN LAUN"

"To speak or not to speak": This is my souvenir of my illegal
visit to Hungary by bicycle.

"Let's see what's down here": Exploring the pyramids of
Teotihuacan, Mexico. Behind me is the Pyramid of the Sun—
the 7th largest pyramid in the world.

Exploring a jungle-enshrouded trail at the Mayan ruins of Coba in Mexico.

"Don't be a Sheep": My guard Molla and I exchange roles at the Simien Highlands, Ethiopia.

The beginning of the road into Theth, Albania.

Theth, Albania: Land of Fairies

"Ah, spring!" Gwen and I mountain biking in the Middle Atlas mountains near Ifrane, Morocco—the beautiful, little-known region where I lived for 11 years.

Doing a track stand (stationary balance) at the edge of a cliff above "Fox Bowl"—a cedar-encircled volcanic cone (at left) in the Middle Atlas mountains of Morocco.

The largest population of endangered Barbary macaques lives in Ifrane, Morocco. Its gorgeous habitat is being degraded by illegal cedar logging and oak burning to make charcoal.

Two untouristed countries I highly recommend are Romania and Slovenia. This is Peleş Castle near Sinaia, Romania.

Inside a local home near Breb, Romania. This woman has spent decades hand-embroidering all you see behind us; they are her family heirlooms.

Bled, Slovenia.

Admiring the turquoise waters of the Soča River, Slovenia. This river is world famous among kayakers but practically unknown to the run-of-the-mill tourist.

PART THREE: EXPLORE LIKE A GLOBAL NOMAD

CHAPTER TEN

"Let's see what's down here."

"The perfect journey is never finished. The goal is always just across the next river, round the shoulder of the next mountain. There is always one more track to follow, one more mirage to explore."—Rosita Forbes

"Go outside and play!" my Mum frequently shouted at me when I complained of being bored during my middle school summer vacations. Because of her command, I began to explore the scattered patches of forest around our suburban home, frequently getting myself into (and out of) some pretty messy situations. These small adventures often ended with me going off-trail with my bike, pushing it through thorn bushes and muddy streams to find my way out of the woods. More often than not, I would come home sweaty, with sloshing sneakers, with arms and legs lacerated and itchy, and with a smile on my face.

As an adult, Mum's command still rings in my head. The difference now is that the adventures are bigger and the messy situations are more dangerous, but they are still just as much fun. These "Adventures with Kolin," as I call them, sometimes entail a little bit of pain and some minor injury, but they make for good stories to tell my friends when I make it back alive. On the other hand, there are just as many occasions when everything goes right. Either way, the exploration is always worth it.

These unpredictable jaunts into the unknown usually start when I spot an appealing path in the forest or a quaint alley in some corner of a city, then say to myself or my travel partner, "Let's see what's down here." Then the adventure begins. The journey can progress in either of two ways:

A: The trail becomes increasingly rocky, steep, thorny, or precipitous...or all of the above; or the dark alley leads to the unsavory bowels of the city, yet I bull-headedly press on, not wanting to backtrack to safety because I've come too far already, and I'm sure a way out is just around the corner. Or...

B: The trail or alley becomes ever more delightful at each turn, revealing glorious natural or architectural beauty and hidden secrets I never would have fathomed, and when I get back to where I started, I think, "Wow! I'm glad I explored the road less traveled!"

If choice "A" doesn't sound like your idea of fun, and you don't care about impressing your friends with tales of derring-do at the risk of life or limb, then may I suggest to you this succinct rule for exploration: **Know when to backtrack.** There have been many instances when I wish I had followed this rule myself because it can get you out of a heap of trouble.

For example, while exploring the magnificent ruins of Teotihuacan near Mexico City, in the corner of my eye I spied a lonely, little-worn trail that called out to me, "Kolin! Come and see what's down here!" The dusty path meandered through brittle yellow grass and disappeared behind a pyramid. Should I venture into the mysterious backstage of Teotihuacan or follow the well-worn tourist trail?

At this point of decision, I usually pause, look around and think to myself, "Why isn't anyone else walking on this trail? What is wrong with all these tourists? They are just like sheep—blindly following each other's tail. Don't they know how to open their eyes and see the boundless opportunities that might be theirs by exploring the unknown? I *know* I'm going to see something cool if I walk down here. I just know it!"

As I glanced disdainfully at the ignorant package-tour zombies of Teotihuacan who mindlessly followed their gaudy guide, my heart skipped a beat when I imagined the pre-Columbian treasures I would discover down this slithering trail. With each dusty step my excitement grew, eagerly expecting to see some ancient pottery shard or sword hilt jutting from beneath crumbling pyramid blocks.

I did find crumbling pyramid blocks and plenty of them. The backside of one pyramid had caved in, forming a black cave filled with jumbled piles of brick, but no artifacts. I thought the cave would be the highlight of my side trip until I saw the spider.

I almost ran into this spider with my chest. As I turned from the cave to continue down the path, I jerked back just in time to avoid a hefty thread of spider web at my neck, stretching for at least three feet (one meter) from one tall blade of grass to another. After taking a moment to marvel at the monstrosity of this trap, I suddenly noticed the equally monstrous owner—a green and yellow arachnid with an abdomen as plump as my thumb and with long toothpick legs—just a few centimeters from my chest. One more step and I would have been intimately acquainted with a new friend.

My first thought was that it would be no big deal to walk around one spider and its web. No matter how large, I wasn't going to let a single spider interfere with my mission of exploration. But as I looked beyond this spider's lair to the sprawling acres of grass beyond, I noticed that I would have to navigate a minefield of closely spun webs to continue down my chosen path. There were hundreds of eight-legged beasties guarding the center of their volleyball nets. It seemed like all the gigantic spiders of Teotihuacan had chosen this untrampled field as their holy site for insect sacrifice.

After assessing the daunting and unending obstacles before me, I decided to keep going. That was when I should have turned back. But in typical "Adventures with Kolin" fashion, I decided that playing Twister with fanged fauna would be an intriguing challenge. Weaving under, around and over this maze of webs soon became a gymnastic routine akin to avoiding laser beams in a booby trapped room. I was sweating profusely from contorting my torso at ungainly angles. After about 30 minutes of gingerly mincing through arachnid alley, I looked ahead to find that I had worked my way out of the spiders' field and smack into my next obstacle: thorn bushes.

I didn't feel like stopping to smell the thorn bush flowers, no matter how pretty their myriad white blossoms were. I now had two choices—spend another half hour twisting my way back through the webs or plow through the spiked thicket before me. I chose the thorns.

After 15 minutes of self-flagellation, I began to believe that sometimes the road less traveled is less traveled for a reason. In fact, there was no road or path to be seen anymore. My dreams of discovering treasure had evaporated under the hot Mexican sun. Now I was in survival mode. I just wanted to get out!

Finally, the thorn bushes ended at a nine foot (three meter) high chicken wire fence topped with barbed wire. The barbed wire was strung between metal posts jutting away from me at a 45 degree angle. On the other side of the fence was a road—the road to freedom, and hopefully a road leading back into the Teotihuacan complex so that I could catch my bus back to Mexico City at 4:30 p.m.

I have experience climbing fences and walls. To get from point A to point B in the most expedient fashion, sometimes a wall or fence must be climbed. But I had never climbed a fence topped with barbed wire. I wasn't about to backtrack through the thorns and the spiders when all that stood between me and freedom was this fence. So I began climbing.

Before climbing any fence from the inside of a perimeter, it is prudent to observe if there are any supporting wires or fence-post struts that you can put your feet on to help you climb up. This fence had none. In this case, the only way to climb up is to get a firm grip with your fingers hooked through the fence above your head and then press the soles of your feet flat against the wire and walk up, or, if possible, stick the toes of your shoes into the polygonal holes in the wire as footholds.

Be sure that when you begin climbing a fence, you climb next to a fence post. This fence post will be very useful as a stabilizer upon which to rest your foot or hand as you psyche yourself up to launch your legs over the top in one arcing jump. This particular fence made jumping over a little more difficult because once I reached the top of the chicken wire, I still had to gingerly step upward and outward from one wobbly barbed wire to the next until my right foot was on the top wire and my right hand was firmly gripping the end of an angled post.

Before jumping, while I tried to calm my trembling legs, I picked a spot on the ground free of rocks, branches or anything else that might twist my ankle or break my leg when I landed. Next, I visualized how I was going to simultaneously push my body's weight off my right foot while swinging my trailing left leg up and over the three strands of barbed wire, hopefully landing on both feet at the same time.

I jumped. I swung my left leg up and over the barbed wire perfectly to join my right leg in the descent. The only problem was that my right *hand* didn't join the rest of my body in the descent quite so readily. My right hand was the last body part to break contact with the fence because it was the fulcrum upon which my body rotated. Thus, while my legs and torso were descending, my right hand still had a light grip on the fence post above my head until my right arm was fully extended. There was a snag in my jump when my right wrist briefly got stuck on a rusty barb which tore a gash in my wrist below my thumb.

"When was my last tetanus shot?" was the first question that flashed in my mind after my feet hit the ground. I couldn't remember. Dying of tetanus in Mexico City was not how I had planned to end my vacation. A warm red stream trickled down my palm as I walked toward a roadside restaurant to ask about a place to wash my wound. A portly, jovial woman tsk-tsk-ed my bloody wrist and pointed to a sink on the outside wall. There was even a bar of gritty, dust-filmed soap! What luck! I pulled my wound apart and, with my fingernail, meticulously scraped every grain of rust out of my wrist under running water then washed my hands and wrist thoroughly with the gritty soap.

On the bus back to Mexico City, with my bloody wrist slowly crusting over, my stomach knotted as I worried about the date of my last tetanus shot. "Perhaps I should have backtracked when I saw the spiders. If only I hadn't gone down that winding path in the first place." Ah! These what-if wonderings were useless! If I hadn't gone down that path, I would forever after regret not exploring my surroundings to the fullest. In the very least, my ordeal would make a good story to tell friends when I got back.

◆ ◆ ◆

Another misadventure began with a seemingly innocuous climb up a hill in China. My Chinese friend Fred and I were spending a few summer days with a Kazakh family in a ramshackle hut next to a rushing river in the Tiān Shān (Heavenly Mountains) of Xinjiang Province. One evening, about two hours before sunset, I told Fred that I wanted to do a little exploring by climbing a forested hill near our shack. Fred said, "OK. Have fun," and I set off into the unknown. I hiked above the tree line then began scaling a scrabbly rock face, not paying attention to where the climb was leading me. My only goal was to get to the top, so I followed my general rule: **When climbing an unknown mountain with no obvious trail, up is good and down is bad.**

In this case, up soon became bad when I found myself on a ledge the width of my foot with my chest and face plastered to the rock and my arms hugging the outwardly bulging cliff. Ahead of me I could see that the ledge I was following got wider just after the next concave corner of the cliff. I inched my way over to the corner until the ledge ran out. There was nothing left to stand on. To get to the other side, I realized that I would have to take a giant step off my ledge onto what appeared to be a triangular, moss-covered shelf of rock that fitted into the concavity of the cliff. The shelf seemed substantially thick—perhaps thick enough to support my 135 pounds (60 kilos)—so I gingerly stretched out my right leg and leaned my weight onto the moss. The shelf held. I reluctantly relinquished my grasp of the cliff as I crouched down to get a handful of mossy tuft and then slid my left foot over onto the shelf. I slowly crab-walked my way toward the middle of the shelf, trying not to think of the 30 foot (ten meter) fall to the rocks below me.

As I inched toward the middle of the shelf, I began to wonder what exactly was supporting this mossy carpet. I suddenly had my answer as my foot broke through the moss and plunged into thin air. A sharp chill pierced my brain with the shocking realization that I was standing on a shelf of intertwined moss roots suspended above a precipice by the tenuous grasp of the outer plants that clung to the rock! This was when I began to pray.

I was so grateful to get off that cliff that I practically skipped back toward the shack. At least I thought I was heading toward the shack. In fact, after climbing down the opposite side of the cliff from where I went up, I had become a bit lost. I knew the approximate direction of the cabin, so I headed down the hill, following my general rule: **When descending an unknown mountain without an obvious trail, down is good and up is bad.**

Down soon became bad. It was getting dark, and I had found a goat trail that led through a rocky, sparsely wooded valley next to a trickling stream. Any outdoorsman worth his salt knows that when you are lost in the woods, your best choice is to follow a waterway since water follows the path of least resistance. Since I knew that my Kazakh family's shack was near a rushing river, I logically assumed that this little stream would lead into that very same river. Once I found that river, I could follow it downstream to the shack.

In my half jovial, half worried mood, I hurried down the goat trail at a good clip, trying to beat the dark. I had no flashlight, no food and no water. All I was wearing were football shorts, a sweat-stained t-shirt and sport sandals. When I left Fred, I didn't think that this little jaunt would take long, and I didn't think that anything could go wrong. But something had already gone wrong and now I was lost...kind of. Little did I know there was more excitement in store.

Before I explain the misfortune that befell me, you must understand that the *Tīan Shān* are blanketed with goats. The *Tīan Shān* are like the Swiss Alps of China. It is a prime location to graze your flocks on bountiful meadows watered by glacier-fed streams. What you also must understand is that a single goat poops a lot. And when you have a lot of goats, you have a proportionate abundance of poop on the trail. The path I was walking was no exception. The rich, soft blackness under my feet was a healthy toe-deep mixture of moist, warm earth and crushed poo balls.

As I heartily strode along, I paid little attention to the rocks rolling underfoot as I surveyed the valley ahead, searching for an opening that would indicate the stream's mouth where it met the river. Suddenly, I stumbled in the dark and sliced the side of my foot on the knife-edge of a jutting rock. The gash didn't even have time to bleed because my next step into the deep, dung-filled dirt plastered my cut with a poultice of black excrement.

I couldn't waste time stopping to clean the cut. I had to find the river and the hut before complete darkness set in. Besides, it would be no use to clean the cut when my next step down the goat trail would paste my wound with mud again. I would have to wait until I got back to the shack to wash.

"What if the poop gets into my bloodstream?" I wondered. "Will I get some kind of mad-goat disease?" I pushed these worrisome thoughts away as I pressed on to find the river.

Finally, I found the river and followed it downstream until I reached the shack. Fred said he was happy to see me because the Kazakh father had gone to look for me on the hill. Fred said he wasn't worried, but the father was since it was now almost completely dark and I hadn't shown up yet. The Kazakh's son Baozhan yelled to his father to come home since the foreigner had returned safely. When the father emerged from the woods and saw me sitting by the fire, he gave me a good scolding like any father would give to his reckless son. Fred translated the Chinese for me, telling me the father said, "It is dangerous for you to go up there! You don't know the mountain and you could get hurt!" I hung my head in mock shame and humbly apologized for troubling the father. He harrumphed his way back to the shack as I now turned my attention to my poop-smeared foot.

I hadn't started to bleat yet, so I wasn't as worried as before about mad-goat disease. But what about infection? I stepped inside the musty shack to retrieve my headlamp from my backpack, then walked over to the only source of water near the shack—the glacier-fed river that roiled over boulders in a frightening froth of chilling whiteness. The trouble was finding a quiet pool with enough of a current to gently clean all the poop out of the gash in my left foot. With my headlamp's beam shining on my blackened foot, I gently wiped away the outer layers of gunk. For the first time I could see the length and depth of the cut— about two inches (five centimeters) long and a quarter inch (half a centimeter) deep. I pulled the flesh open and let the flowing water flush every fleck of feces from my foot.

My next problem was that my cut wouldn't stop bleeding. The ice water had numbed my foot so my blood was too cold to coagulate. I sat on my riverside boulder watching a thin but constant red stream pour from my cut while I waited for my foot to warm. I had no bandages, so hopefully my sock and shoe would keep any further dirt from entering my wound. Eventually, my foot warmed up, my blood started to clot, I put on my socks and shoes, and walked back to the fireplace to eat supper.

The next day, Fred and I left the shack's mountain heights for the much lower parking lot of Heavenly Lake (*Tiān Chí*) from where we had started our adventure. All during the rocky, three-hour hike I could feel my cut breaking open with each bend of my foot.

♦ ♦ ♦

You mustn't let fear of minor injury stop you from exploring, no! Misadventures like the two above happen only half the time I explore. Many wonderful discoveries can be made when you tell yourself, **"Let's see what's down here."** For this reason, don't dissuade yourself from wandering into the dank, clinging shadows of that root-tangled jungle path before you.

There is no better place to find such a path as in the Yucatan peninsula—Mexico's rainforest treasury of astounding Mayan ruins nestled under a verdant umbrella. If you visit one of these sites in the early morning or late evening, the tourist-free silence lets you imagine you are the first to re-discover a long-forgotten civilization. This precious solitude at the ruins of Coba heightened the magic of my search for an ancient *sacbe*.

The word sacbe (plural *sacbeob*) is Yucatec Maya for "white road." The *sacbeob* were raised limestone roads usually joining buildings within a temple complex, but sometimes much longer *sacbeob* joined different sites. The 60 mile (100 kilometer long *sacbe* joining Coba to Yaxuna was the longest one known to archaeologists for decades, and it was this *sacbe* that I was determined to find.

As I ambled down the shaded promenades of Coba, I kept an eye out for any significant path that looked like it might be the *sacbe* to Yaxuna. That I had no clue what direction Yaxuna lay did not bother me one bit. I wasn't fazed in the least by the lack of any *sacbe* marked on the tourist map of Coba. No matter what lay ahead, I was determined to leave the tourist trail yet again. This time I just knew I was going to discover something more worthwhile than spiders, thorns and barbed wire.

The thought that today I might walk on the same pre-Columbian road that Mayan priests and warriors, mothers and children, traders and wanderers had walked enraptured me. I was alone in the Yucatan rainforest amid the buzzing of flies and the occasional squawk of a toucan, enjoying the humid shade and the wonder that if I found this *sacbe* I could keep walking for 60 miles (100 kilometers) before I emerged from the jungle at my destination.

At the tree-lined perimeter of one temple, I noticed a yellow police-barrier type of tape stretching across an unnaturally large gap between two trees. As I peered past the tape into the forest beyond, I perceived a patch of white on the ground reflecting a ray that pierced the jungle canopy. I nonchalantly glanced around to be sure that no tourist or caretaker was nearby before I ducked under the tape and walked to the white rock I saw gleaming in the sun.

A large limestone slab, about three feet (a meter) long and a foot (30 centimeters) wide, jutted above the leaf litter by about two inches (five centimeters). This first slab—rectangular, unevenly worn but smooth-surfaced—lay flush to another similar slice followed by another, and then another for as far as I could see through the undergrowth that draped the white way. As I eagerly stepped upon the ancient paving stone, I half feared this path would peter out like the trail at Teotihuacan. But this road was so solid and unerring in its straightness. The weathered white stones, peeking through the embrace of cloying roots, guided me as I marched ever deeper into the vibrant jungle and ever farther from the pallid ruins of Coba.

CHAPTER ELEVEN

Don't Be a Sheep

*"The one who follows the crowd
will usually get no further than
the crowd. The ones who walk
alone are likely to find themselves
in places no one has ever been
before." –Albert Einstein*

*"Make yourselves sheep and the
wolves will eat you."
–Benjamin Franklin*

M ost people are like sheep. They mindlessly and unquestioningly follow everyone else because it is easy.

They lack originality or the guts or the knowledge to do things differently than everyone else.

Let me give you an example of what I mean: Have you ever noticed that wherever a line is forming—at the bank, at the airport check-in aisle, at the cinema ticket window—everyone seems to stand in the same line? No one ever bothers to check if there is another window or clerk available next to the mass of people standing in that one line. More often than not, I have found that there is in fact a very bored looking person sitting behind a window or desk with absolutely no one standing in front of them. That is great news for me, and too bad for the sheep! I get served at the bank or airport or movie theater first and leave all the sheep bleating discontentedly in line.

I could expand this comparison of people being like sheep to question how people in developed countries live their lives: do we have to follow the prescribed formula that life=school then job then marriage then children? Should people look down on those who choose to travel before looking for a job? What about those who work to live rather than live to work? Is there really anything wrong with those who don't want to marry or who don't want to have children or who marry late and adopt children? Why not live out your "retirement" now while you are young and healthy rather than waiting until your body is decrepit to finally take a break from work to enjoy life?

I could use the unquestioning attitude of sheep to critique what is "normal" in education: is academic learning, which traditionally appeals to only the linguistically and mathematically intelligent, appropriate for every student? Shouldn't there be more schools for people whose strengths are the other intelligences (spatial, intra- and interpersonal, kinesthetic, musical)? Shouldn't young people be encouraged more to follow their dreams rather than the "practical" stable jobs?

But since this book is about travel, can I apply this sheep metaphor to travelers? Absolutely! Don't be a sheep when you travel, either. What I mean is:

Kolin's Anti-Sheep Travel Rule: Don't travel where everyone else travels.

Okay, so you don't want to miss out on Paris and Rome and Tokyo and London and New York and all those other famous cities. Go on and get those out of your system first. Now don't get me wrong. I don't mean to belittle these famous locations. I've been there and done that, and I have to admit that those places have their merits: There is no greater palace in the world than Versailles, there is no more magnificent cathedral than St. Peters, and there is no other clock tower so famously misidentified as "Big Ben" than the Elizabeth Tower at the Houses of Parliament in London. The world's most visited cities are full of marvelous monuments, museums and architecture.

Go and see the Louvre and Pisa's crooked campanile and the Köln cathedral, but don't miss out on the charming, colorful buildings and cobblestoned streets of Guanajuato, Mexico and Sighişoara, Romania. Don't forget to visit the bucolic beauties of Banska Štiavnica, Slovakia and Bled, Slovenia. Mostar's Stari Most is more scenic and just as historic as Prague's Karlovy Most, and the walled cities of Dali, China and Počitelj, Bosnia and Herzegovina are worthy rivals of Ávila, Spain. There is no other monastery more intriguingly painted and scenically situated than Rila Monastery in Bulgaria. And these are just a few of the world's little-known but fascinating man-made attractions. I haven't even begun to expound on the natural wonders that few people ever visit.

For example, have you hiked through Vikos Gorge in northern Greece or rafted on the aquamarine waters of the Tara River in Montenegro? You must go swimming with the dourados in the crystalline rivers of Bonito, Brazil! There is no greater waterfall in volume, length and ambiance than Iguaçu on the border of Argentina and Brazil—not even Victoria is so grand or scenic. There is no cave more stupendously decorated (and accessible to the public) than Postojna in Slovenia. Having a huge griffin vulture flap just above your head at Serbia's sinuous Uvac River Gorge is a rare experience in a seldom visited but beautiful location. I could go on for hours.

Besides the intrinsic benefits of seeing a memorable place or experiencing a new culture or activity in these little-known places, what are the other benefits of traveling off the usual backpacker circuits and trampled tourist trails?

Anti-sheep Reason #1: Bragging rights.
How many people do you know who can say that they have ridden in a yellow submarine in the ocean off Jeju Island or eaten *chapulines* in Oaxaca or sat among puffins above the Arctic circle near Iceland? Of course you don't want to gloat over your travel superiority with your friends, but think of all the fascinating experiences you will be able to share with them.

Anti-sheep Reason #2 : You will have the whole place to yourself.
There are no bull-horn toting Chinese guides with their meek flocks wearing matching neon-orange baseball caps at the wooden churches surrounding Breb, Romania. You won't have to jostle shoulder to shoulder, pushing against summer tourist hordes as you stroll the shores of Aurlandsfjord in Flåm, Norway as you would strolling the canals of Venice. You won't miss the crowds as you shop for culturally authentic hand-crafted souvenirs along the narrow streets of Etar, Bulgaria. Even in the heart of over-loved

Switzerland at the height of tourist season you can enjoy the isolated serenity of a two-day walk on the Alp's largest glacier— the Aletsch.

Anti-sheep Reason #3: You are the boss of your own time and destinations.

Unless you are elderly, an extremely anxious traveler, or it is your first time overseas, please don't take a pre-planned package tour. If you are somewhat familiar with traveling, then try seeing the world on your own or with one good friend and choose some out-of-the-way locations. If you are going to go where no one else goes, then there probably won't be many package tours anyway, and your adventure will be all the more memorable for it.

When you plan your trip yourself, you are the boss and not the guide. You are in control of your destination choices. This means that you should research the locations you most want to visit. Read your guidebook from cover to cover, dog ear those pages, highlight and underline those details that spark your interest most. You will become a better-informed and more culturally sensitive tourist because of your research before you even step foot in that country.

Second, when you plan your trip yourself, you are in control of your time and not the guide. You won't have to spend only 15 minutes at Jerusalem's Wailing Wall because that is all the time the guide allowed you. No. You will be able to take a deep breath, leisurely look around you and take in all the sights, sounds and smells. You will have the time to ponder the meaning of such devotion and listen to the tear-filled prayers of the devotees. You won't have to rush around taking photos as souvenirs because your brain can't adequately take it all in before the guide yells at you to return to the bus.

To further whet your appetite for adventurous travel in unheard-of places, I would like to introduce to you three treasures that made a lasting impression on me. The first place is in Ethiopia where I saw endemic and unusual wildlife and had an intriguing human encounter. To visit the second location is to step back in time. This tiny Albanian mountain village is as culturally isolated as it is physically by the almost oppressive mountains that encircle it. The final location was my home for 11 years—Ifrane, Morocco—a place blessed with unappreciated natural beauty.

LOCATION ONE: SIMIEN HIGHLANDS, ETHIOPIA

I had never held a weapon before. Its dull metal and lifeless wood felt evil. As the gun lay firmly in my hands, its solid weight crept coldly up my arms, squeezed my chest with a gasp, then sat upon my heart with the chill ache of death. To my left, the owner of this Kalashnikov smiled beatifically at my awkwardness, then nervously fingered the camera that hung obtrusively around his neck.

♦ ♦ ♦

One week ago, I had arrived in Addis Ababa, Ethiopia. On a whim, I visited an orthodox cathedral just before catching a plane to Gondar where I thought our adventure would begin. But the adventure had already begun here, in a place of worship so unfamiliar to me with all its vibrant, gaudy paintings of a very brown-skinned Ethiopian-looking holy family plastering every inch of every wall. This was no majestically reserved European cathedral. The decorations here flamboyantly proclaimed Ethiopia's long historical link to the Holy Land, not least of which being the mysterious claim that the Ark of the Covenant was secretly hidden here.

A disembodied male voice soared to the church's blue dome studded with golden stars. His sacred song lilted to the slow, soothing accompaniment of the masenko, Ethiopia's traditional one-stringed lute, making me realize, in an almost spiritual, other-worldly way, that I had definitely arrived in a country like no other I had visited before.

But I had come to visit a cathedral of a different kind. With my cousin Natalie and her friend John, both medical NGO workers stationed in Kenya, I planned to visit one of nature's grandest sanctuaries: the colossal pinnacles and sky-scraping plateaus of the Simien Highlands. Our three-day trek would never stoop below 9000 feet (3000 meters) and we relished the chance to glimpse some of Ethiopia's endemic wildlife along the way.

Seeing my name on a sign as I exited Gondar's airport was a relief, and to see a warm beaming smile above that sign was a pleasure. Jemal Hussien, our guide, invited us to hop in a slightly outdated but fully functional Toyota Land Cruiser painted a cheery lemon yellow from the windows to the roof. The gigantic luggage rack held three large plastic barrels filled with our drinking water for the three day trek, a burly spare tire and who knew what else under that lumpy blue tarp. Our backpacks were crammed in the back of the Land Cruiser next to—who would have guessed?—a handsome young man holding an AK-47 machine gun.

Molla was our personal body guard for this trip, though what he was guarding us from I wasn't quite sure. I suppose it was from bandits or maybe the wild animals? But whenever I glanced at Molla's serene smile and glistening chestnut eyes, I had no doubt that he was too kindhearted to kill an ant. I felt sorry that he was so squished by our supplies, but Molla seemed perfectly content squatting silently upon his luggage throne. I just hoped he would keep that gun pointed at the ceiling, especially if we hit a bump in the road.

Sometimes asphalt, mostly dirt like powdered cinnamon, the road to the highlands carved through the endless amber of teff fields. Past cylindrical mud-brick homes, we wended ever higher until we reached our drop off point. The supplies and our packs were loaded on mules by coy, slinking muleteers as Jemal, Natalie, John and I set off for our first trek in the Simien toward Sankaber camp at 9000 feet (3000 meters). Somewhere behind us sauntered lackadaisical Molla, his rifle casually slung over one shoulder as he shuffled along in his black Adidas beach sandals.

Natalie worried that she wouldn't be able to hike at this altitude. She had never been this high before and it had been almost a year since she had last been hiking. But Jemal's leisurely gait set the pace for a very manageable hike from first day to last, and Natalie was pleasantly surprised that after the first day at altitude she managed the following two days with no serious trouble.

Trees were sparse on the plateau, but the trees I saw weren't trees at all! One of them was a giant heather, appearing as if a transplanted shrub of the Scottish Highlands had defied the thinning oxygen to mutate into a monstrous moss-bearded behemoth. The other "tree" was a flowering plant—the giant lobelia. This amazing plant has a single rosette of hard cactus-like leaves that grow for several decades, putting all their energy into producing a colossal flower up to nine feet (three meters) tall. Actually, the "flower" is a towering cork-like finger pointing to the sky encircled from top to bottom by row upon row of lilac tongues—each tongue an individual flower. The giant lobelia flowers once, and then dies.

As we crested a rise, we were slowly and silently engulfed by a horde of intimidating primates with eye-catching, bleeding-heart stains on their chests, electrified hair that shot up and out from their faces, and canines larger than a lion's. Perhaps this is why Molla carried a machine gun. Shouldn't Molla have his rifle ready and aimed at these eccentric monkeys? I glanced around, but Molla was nowhere to be seen. Fortunately, this time there was no need to worry: we had wandered into a very accommodating troop of gelada baboons as they placidly grazed like miniature hirsute cows.

Geladas are the only primates whose diet is mostly grass and their hands are well suited to the task; they have the most highly opposed thumbs of any primate other than humans making it easy for them to delicately pick grass blade by blade until they have a good fistful to stuff into their menacing mouths.

I quietly sauntered along with the geladas until I could sit myself among the thick of the advancing baboons. Geladas, endemic to Ethiopia, are highly social with groups sometimes numbering in the hundreds. I felt like one of the family (after all, I am hairy enough). The baboons didn't even give me a second look as if it was nothing unusual for me to be within a couple of feet (half a meter) of some of the larger males. The silence was only broken by the tearing sound of baboons mowing the lawn and an occasional rhythmic grunt as the grazing primates passed within arm's reach.

Jamal quietly told us that this low, soft grunt is given when one baboon approaches another with friendly intentions. I guess it was like saying, "Hey, Kolin, I'm now entering your personal space, so don't get testy." The male baboons didn't need to worry about me. After seeing one male flip back his upper lip to aggressively show off his massive fangs, I wasn't going to make any startling moves that might precipitate a bite. If I were attacked by a baboon, that would be a time when I would need Molla's protection, but he was nowhere to be seen.

What if we did need Molla's protection? Would he be in the right place at the right time? Until now he had kept his distance, slowly materializing from behind a giant heather tree and then disappearing behind a giant lobelia. And who was Molla, really? Had he fought in a war? Was he married? Did he have children? What did he think of tourists like me who came to visit his country? Like the muleteers, Molla was one of those silent, little-noticed locals who made my trip run smoothly. He was my invisible guardian—always present but seldom seen.

I think my curiosity about Molla stemmed from the incongruity of his soothing, coffee-brown good looks and the harsh Russian lines of the deadly steel he carried. But my questions remained unanswered for now because we didn't share a language. How could I approach Molla to establish rapport before I peppered Jemal with questions about my reticent guard?

Just before sunset we reached Sankaber, our tents already pitched with down sleeping bags unfurled inside, and chunky vegetable soup boiling in the pot. The night was cold, and I needed my wool beanie to protect my bald head from the chill, but I soon dozed off with a happy belly and memorable moments feeding my sweet dreams.

Breakfast in the sun was a glorious way to meet the morning. As the sun warmed our faces, steaming thermoses of hot milk and coffee warmed our insides. Some pied crows and thick-billed ravens came begging for crumbs, and we obliged. After breakfast, there was no need to take down our tents or roll up our sleeping bags. The small army of muleteers took care of all that. All we had to do was fill our water bottles, swing on our daypacks, and off we marched toward our second camp, Geech, at 10,800 feet (3600 meters).

A hurricane of flapping wings rose from the high grass before us. We had startled a lammergeyer, one of my favorite birds. These gargantuan bearded vultures can have a wingspan of up to nine feet (three meters) and the one we scared was grand. It seemed quite an effort at first for the heavy bird to get off the ground, but once its wings caught the wind, this beautiful scavenger rose swiftly until it was a speck in the sky.

"A vulture can be beautiful?" you might ask. Well, the lammergeyer is a vulture unlike any other, lacking the bald head, neck and legs, and the generally disheveled look of most other vultures. Golden brown feathers cover the legs, chest and head; its wings and back are black; it has a white face with a red eye circle and a black stripe across its cheek which ends in a goatee worth of Errol Flynn.

The majestic lammergeyer isn't endemic to the Simien Highlands, but it is definitely a haven for them. Besides the gelada, other endemic species are Menelik's bushbuck and the Ethiopian wolf, the world's rarest canid and Africa's most endangered carnivore. Other distinctive wildlife you might be lucky to see are the Nubian ibex and the secretary bird. On this trip we counted ourselves lucky to get up close and personal with the geladas, to admire the gliding lammergeyers, and to spot one Menelik's bushbuck from a distance as it wandered by our campsite at Sankaber.

The next morning the burnished sky blazed blue through the gaps in the giant heather branches. We had arrived at Imet Gogo, a scenic overlook at 12,000 feet (3926 meters). For the first time, Molla was at our side peering with us at the collected grains of salt that were villages below.

Suddenly, I had an idea. I knew how I would break the silent barrier between Molla and me. Through Jemal, I asked Molla to please come and take a photo with me, but with one special request: I wanted to switch roles with him. I would hold the rifle and Molla would wear my DSLR camera. That is how I came to grasp a Kalashnikov for the first time. To see Molla smile at the humor of our role reversal made this brief encounter more than just a photo souvenir. It became a longed-for chance to open a conversation with my invisible guardian.

Through Jemal, I learned that Molla lived in the village of Mekarebia with his wife and five children. His Kalashnikov was his weapon during the Eritrean-Ethiopian War and Molla's military training was a necessary requirement to be employed by Simien National Park. Jemal said that we needed Molla to protect us from bandits who might attack our small trekking group, but Jemal assured us that during his 13 years as a guide no such attack had ever happened. The most important reason for having Molla along was to employ the local population so that they could benefit from foreign tourist income.

Jemal had saved the best view for last: At Imet Gogo's edge, the world fell away at my feet. Skirting the edge of a vertiginous cliff, I marveled at the massive eroded molars which rose from half a mile (a kilometer) below. Though it was hazy, we could see a never-ending perspective of layered, angular ridges silhouetted against a cold, anemic sky. Tufts of blond grass swished frantically in powerful chilly updrafts.

A lammergeyer-shaped speck soared hundreds of meters below me, the bird itself still infinitely higher than the white dots that were villages below. A blond blob of gelada blended with the tufted grass on an impossible foothold to my right. The wind lifted Molla's voice as he sang a haunting tune to the void. In this moment, I knew I had found a place like no other.

LOCATION TWO: THETH, ALBANIA

The guidebook said I shouldn't attempt driving down the 11-mile (18-kilometer) dirt road into the valley of Theth without a four-wheel-drive vehicle. I ignored the warning and crossed over the "Accursed Mountains," as the Albanian Alps are called, in my rental sedan, telling myself "It isn't that bad" all the way to the valley bottom. Where the asphalt ended, a rutted mud two-track hung above a precipice with only a foot (30 centimeters) of road to spare from the outer edge of my passenger-side tires. Trying to enjoy the majestic view and ignore the knot slowly forming in my stomach, I inched my car along the edge of the cliff. It wasn't that bad. Then it only took me an hour and a half of slow maneuvering over menacing rocks that wanted to rip open my muffler. It wasn't so bad. I only once had to drive through a river formed by a waterfall that fell down a cliff next to my car. The water only covered my tires. It wasn't that bad. But after four days of non-stop rain, I began to wonder "What if the road has turned to a soupy mess? What if I'm stuck here?"

But what an enchanting place to be stuck! I was now in the land of *zane*—mountain fairies who lived in caves. In local lore, a *zana* would appear as an alluring woman bathing naked in a crystal stream. But don't be mistaken: in Albania, the fairies are brave and valiant opponents who can give special powers to worthy warriors but petrify you with one look if you get on their bad side.

Theth is where the law of *Kanun* still rules; if family honor is sullied, then blood feuds ensue. There is even a handy blood feud tower in the center of the village where you can lock yourself in to keep from being killed by the family members you offended. The sign for tourists outside this bleak stone tower reads exactly thus: "THE DEFENSE TOWER OF THETHI: The place of self security. The guilty person waits the irritability to be substituted by reasonable actions. He bilieves that someone will negotiate for his fault to be judget in justice."

Theth is a village trapped by mountains glimmering with snow—scenery that would make any hiker salivate with anticipation. At least I was pretty sure there were mountains hiding behind the rain. Clouds like crazed sea foam skimmed their soggy skirts over the twitching heather, making tiny Theth feel doubly trapped—by geography and weather. Surely the clouds would part soon so that I could wander the mountain meadows to find a *tulipa albanica*. Or perhaps I could spot a brown bear, fallow dear or wild boar in the primeval forest.

On my final morning, a broad, heart-warming beam of sunlight found a chink in the mountains' armor and slanted across Theth, illuminating the breakfast-fire smoke that curled from the village chimneys. Snow shimmered above the dark, toothy silhouettes of cliffs not yet kissed by the source of life. I gleefully ran outside with camera in hand to glimpse the proud line of mountains that didn't seem so accursed anymore. No. I renamed them the "Blessed Mountains." Now if only they could bless my Fiat Tipo as I drove up their mighty flanks. If only I could be as brave as a fairy...

LOCATION THREE: IFRANE NATIONAL PARK, MOROCCO

There's a green heart to Morocco, pulsing with the fragrance of cedar and fallen oak leaves. A heart brightened by brash paint strokes of wildflowers in spring and livened with birdsong in summer. It beats to the rhythms of Nature, waiting patiently to draw you away from the clichés of Marrakech and Toubkal with its serene temptations. That heart is the Middle Atlas countryside of Ifrane National Park.

Everyone has heard of the High Atlas...but the *Middle Atlas*? Probably not. I have lived in the Middle Atlas for eleven years and I can confidently tell you, after traveling extensively in Morocco, that I wouldn't want to live anywhere else. Ifrane National Park and the town of Ifrane, after which the park is named, are just one and a half hours by car from both Fes and Meknes. Yet the tourists who do stop here only stay for 30 minutes to wander Ifrane's *centre ville* before climbing back into their package-tour coaches. They move on to Merzouga, oblivious that they have missed Ifrane's real attraction. Nevermind. That just means the cedar and oak forests of this park will remain silent and unsullied for me and for you.

During my first two years as a university lecturer in Ifrane, I was the only mountain biker in the area. Then I met Guinevere McWhorter, a new English Literature teacher at the local orphanage. She is an American who loves reading, hiking and mountain biking. I asked her if she would ride with me and she said "Yes!" Great! I had found a mountain biker babe to be my friend.

When I met Gwen at her house for our first ride, her second-hand Scott mountain bike made my Chinese-made all-steel "J-Murray" (cool name, huh?) look like a Fiat Multipla next to a Lamborghini Aventador. But I felt no self-consciousness, oh no. After all, it isn't the bike that matters, it's the trail you take and how you ride it that counts (at least that's what I told myself).

Gwen and I got to know each other on some short mountain bike trips, and I noticed Gwen knew how to ride. On a quick downhill single-track, I watched Gwen as she smoothly weaved her bicycle around shin-high domes of pedal-snagging heather. She knew how to flow with her bike, and I told her so.

The next weekend I planned a longer ride, and called up Gwen to invite her. The destination for that day was the Azrou Cliff—a 100 foot (30 meter) high chunk of rock poking its flat brow above the famous (among Moroccans) Middle Atlas cedar forest overlooking the town of Azrou. I decided not to tell Gwen that there would be 16 miles (25 kilometers) of climbing and 3,300 feet (1000 meters) of total elevation gain during our 30-mile (48 kilometer) round-trip journey. She didn't need to know these details to enjoy the ride.

Gwen and I pedaled out of Ifrane past the turret of King Mohammed VI's castle-palace, and hung a right on the dirt trail that leads into the Ifrane cedar forest. Occasionally we waved at a leather-skinned Berber shepherd herding his flock with his slingshot and his dogs. This slingshot they carry is no Tom Sawyer-ish hand-hewn toy. This is an honest-to-goodness David and Goliath slingshot. You know the kind where one little stone goes into the sling and the sling goes round and round.

Now why do these shepherds carry slingshots? My theory is that the practice harks back to the days when the Middle Atlas lion still haunted the craggy hills and dark cedar forests of Ifrane and Azrou. Just as in biblical times, when shepherd boy David didst slay the lioneth when he flickethed his wrist and madeth the stone to fly (King James Version), so did the Berbers use their slingshots to protect their flocks by night from the roaring lion which prowled around seeking what sheep it might devour. But since the last Atlas lion was killed in 1922, today the Berber shepherds use their slingshots to herd sheep in the right direction by slinging a well-aimed rock at the ground to the left or right of the wayward flock.

Once, on a hike with my friend Thomas, we met a shepherd and I wanted to try his slingshot. Since Thomas speaks Arabic and I don't, Thomas asked the shepherd if he could show us how to use his weapon. The shepherd, named Omar Aziz, was more than happy to oblige.

The slingshot used by Omar and all other shepherds is a five to six-foot (two meter) long length of chord with a leather pouch in the middle. On one end of this chord is a loop of string that you must slip over the little finger of your throwing hand. This loop of string will keep you from throwing the whole slingshot with the rock when you open your hand. The loose end of the chord will fly open, releasing the rock, while the looped end will remain attached to your little finger.

Next, Omar showed us how to hold both ends of the chord together with your throwing hand so that the slingshot hangs vertically while holding a round stone in the pouch with the other hand. As you begin the first rotation of the slingshot over your head, you can let go of the stone which is now kept in the pouch by momentum. After three whirring swings over his head, Omar opened his hand. The loose end of his slingshot broke the sound barrier as it cracked like a bull whip, sending the stone zinging like a bullet to its mark.

I had my turn next. Just transitioning from holding the stone in the pouch to beginning a swing was harder than it looked. My first shot fizzled in a powerless arc, plopping to the ground only 30 feet (ten meters) away. My next stone didn't go exactly where I thought it would—it somehow flew behind me rather than forward. I wasn't nearly as impressive at the slingshot as a shepherd, but the experience of using an ancient weapon and of meeting Omar the friendly Berber was worth every moment.

After passing two dry lake beds, Gwen and I took a left as we emerged from the Ifrane cedar forest. A dirt road passed the squat rectangles of mud-brick homes overrun with lazy chickens and brown Berber children. Turning left out of the dusty village, we pedaled up the two-mile (three kilometer) hill that would bring us to 5,700 feet (1740 meters), our highest elevation in the Azrou cedar forest.

The Azrou cedar forest is famous for two things: the endangered Barbary macaques and the *Cedre Gouraud*. The Gouraud Cedar *was* the oldest known cedar in the forest, but now it is the *deadest*. Its fame was its demise, for tourists (mostly Moroccan) came to visit in their cars and drove over the tree's shallow roots, thus killing the tree. The bleached behemoth still stands, a sad silhouette of its former glory, and I just can't understand why all the tourists still hang around this dead tree. Really, this made it all the better for me and Gwen, since we had the quiet, wooded trails to ourselves. There is so much forest to explore! There are certainly larger and more beautiful specimens in the forest to admire than the Gouraud Cedar. With a little exploring you can easily find trees 6-10 feet (two to three meters) in diameter.

There are guaranteed sightings of Barbary macaques in the cedar forest around the Gouraud Cedar. Ifrane National Park has the largest population of these endangered primates in the world (Barbary macaques are found only in North Africa and Gibraltar). Feeding the macaques is not advised, but it is a popular pastime with Moroccan tourists. Once you see their fangs when they yawn (the macaques' fangs, not the Moroccans') you will have second thoughts about feeding the loitering, overfed macaques. From previous experience, I knew if Gwen and I rode deeper into the woods away from the crowds, we would find a mellower group of monkeys than the sometimes aggressive beggars that hang around the tourists.

We rode off the established trail into the embrace of the silent cedar sentinels. Only the snapping of twigs below our tires and the occasional haunting call of a Levaillant's green woodpecker broke the quiet. We propped our bikes against a tree and picked a sunny, grassy spot to sit and have a snack. As we ate, the rustle of our plastic food bags soon attracted a lone monkey. He was a skinny guy (I'll call him Ali) and a little wary of us at first. But soon Ali's curiosity and the smell of food compelled him to approach. Ali inched nearer yet never came closer than three feet (a meter). He quietly sat next to me and peered at me with pouting brown eyes. I felt like I had a new friend of the forest to keep me company.

A macaque is a social creature, and soon Ali's buddies Ousama and Brahim came over to bug him. They wrestled and chased and fought for the right to sit as close to me and my food as possible. They reminded me of teenage boys—rambunctious and gangly, still unsure of themselves and their identity in their social hierarchy. A little later, the moms of the gang arrived carrying babies that clung to their mothers' bellies or backs.

Pretty soon, Gwen and I were surrounded by more than thirty macaques who were just minding their own business—tussling and chewing on twigs and grooming each other—while we silently watched and ate our food unmolested. We felt like members of the troupe! But the primate camaraderie didn't last. Suddenly Mounir, the three-foot (one meter) tall alpha male came loping into camp and herded his females away. I quietly said goodbye to Ali and Ousama and Brahim as the teenagers reluctantly left their place next to me and lagged behind their clan like dissatisfied delinquents.

We got back on the trail, and Gwen powered up a gravel hill past a Moroccan man pushing his bike. He looked her way with surprise to see a white foreign woman riding out there in the cedar forest. We sped downhill over a rocky road only to climb again to reach a winding dirt path that skirts the edge of the Azrou Cliff, overlooking the green patchwork wheat fields of the Azrou valley. The view was stupendous, and all around us were fields of pink flowers that we picked and stuck in each other's helmet vents. Ah, spring!

What is the best way to make friends with a Berber, hang with some Barbary macaques and bond with a biker babe named Gwen? Only by mountain biking the Middle Atlas.

◆ ◆ ◆

I hope your sense of adventure was aroused by reading these three stories. Such adventures await you, too, if you follow my advice: Don't be a sheep; be your own shepherd. Leave the tourist flocks behind. Gather up your courage! Go explore the unknown edges of our ever-surprising world.

CHAPTER TWELVE

Dream. Plan. Save. Go.

*"The world is a book and those
who do not travel read only
one page."*
— *Augustine of Hippo*

*"The traveler sees what he sees.
The tourist sees what he has
come to see."*
— *G.K. Chesterton*

The seconds crawled by like a funerary procession. If time went any slower, I thought I might have a near-death experience. In fact, as the meeting stretched into its third hour, my mind left my body behind as I scanned the world map on the wall behind the Dean. Maps always make me think of travel, so as I surveyed Europe, I began to dream of a perfect summer holiday.

"Wah WAH wah, mwah wah wah..."

The Dean's droning became an unintelligible lecture worthy of Charlie Brown's teacher. His mumbling was soon stifled as my summer travel plans swelled with glorious ambition in my mind. By the end of the meeting, I had mentally sketched a rough itinerary that included mountain biking in the French Alps and the Italian Dolomites, visiting the fjordlands of Norway, and hiking on the Isle of Skye.

Then came the hard part. Over the next eight months, I researched the best mountain biking locations in Europe, compared hotels, checked maps, browsed dates and prices on budget airlines, and finally booked all the flights and accommodation for my five-week summer epic. Since I already had the necessary money saved, the only step left was to go! On that trip, I crossed some dreams off my bucket list like biking the Rallarvegen, walking on a glacier, surviving the UCI World Championship Downhill trail at Ft. William, and taking some postcard-worthy snapshots of the Old Man of Storr. None of these goals would have come true if I hadn't fulfilled these four action verbs—dream, plan, save, and go.

Step 1: Dream with a purpose.

It is easy to dream. Anyone can rest their chin in the palm of their hand, gaze out a window and let their mind wander. People imagine themselves lounging on a beach in the Maldives or strolling the streets of Machu Picchu, but that is as far as they get. Soon thoughts from the "real world" come crashing back into their minds like a tidal wave, obliterating their wanderlust. These are thoughts like, "I don't have enough money," "I could never afford that," "I don't have enough holiday time." Or they are plagued with worries like, "What if I get sick while overseas?" "How will I find the time to plan a trip like that?" "I'll fall behind on my work if I take time off," "How will I survive if no one speaks English there?"

Dreaming with a purpose is different. Dreaming with a purpose doesn't allow negative thoughts to stamp your idea to death. When you dream, your purpose should be to hold fast to your goal, believing that with time and effort you can reach your destination. And you must believe that the experience will be worth it.

Dreaming with a purpose is the first step toward commitment, and to fulfill that commitment you will need a plan.

Step 2: Plan with an attitude of flexibility.

Careful attention to detail and flexibility are contradictory. But that is the paradox of travel. No matter how carefully you might plan each day, sometimes life throws a wrench into the machinery of your clockwork plans. For example, my brief stay in Cape Town was to be adrenaline packed, but rain prevented me from rappelling down Table Mountain, fog kept my skydiving plane grounded, and 12 foot (four meter) ocean swells stopped me from cage diving with great white sharks. I was disappointed, but easily found other entertaining diversions to keep me busy.

Short trips from two weeks to a month usually need intense planning to carefully fit in all you want to do between train, bus and plane connections to your next destination. But long trips from one month to a year or more have the luxury of ample time to plan as you go along.

For example, my "seven month summer" of 2008 began with very little planning at all. It started when I finished my high school teaching job in Indonesia and flew to the U.S for a job interview. To my chagrin, the interview was cancelled, and I was left jobless. With money saved from my job in Indonesia and a ticket to Salt Lake City (where the interview would have been) I began a two month journey around the U.S and Canada visiting old friends while seeing Moab, Crater Lake, Olympic National Park, and Isle Royale along the way.

When I finished that tour in Austin, Texas, I decided to take a Greyhound bus to Monterrey, Mexico. After three months of falling in love with Mexico, I booked several flights to get me from Cancun to Dominica. There I spent seven blissful weeks exploring the "Nature Island." As long as there was money in the bank, I kept traveling, taking each day as it came and looking for my next destination in my guidebook whenever I felt the urge to move on.

Whether it is a detailed daily itinerary for a two week trip or a rough outline for a six-month, multi-country journey, the point is that you must have a plan. Without any research about the cost of living, hotel prices, or airfare deals (see Appendix) you won't have any idea of how much money you will need. Which brings us to the next step.

Step 3: Save your money.

For some, this can be the most difficult and discouraging step. The difficulty is in finding ways to save (see appendix), and discouragement comes from the long wait before you have enough money to make the dream trip a reality. But don't give up! Remember Step One—hold onto your dream believing that, in the end, the experience will be worth the effort. Once you have saved the money, then...

Step 4: Go with your eyes and mind wide open.

You've dreamed. You've planned. You've saved all that money. Why are you hesitating? Buy that plane ticket, book your hotels, and go! You won't regret it. As an experienced global nomad, I guarantee that if you go with an open mind, your trip won't only be a relaxing holiday, but also a learning experience. Mark Twain wrote, "Travel is fatal to prejudice, bigotry, and narrow-mindedness, and many of our people need it sorely on these accounts. Broad, wholesome, charitable views of men and things cannot be acquired by vegetating in one little corner of the earth all one's lifetime" (*The Innocents Abroad/Roughing It*). In other words, travel is one of the best ways to broaden your knowledge and positively alter your opinions about the world outside your "little corner." What might you learn on your trip?

First, you could pick up a few useful phrases in the local language. "Where is the _____?" "How much is it?" "May I please have a/some _____?" and learning your numbers up to 100 are all good for starters. Even if you only practice your "please" and "thank you" in the native tongue, it will go a long way in endearing yourself to the locals. Don't be afraid to make mistakes. A little embarrassment is worth the benefits of better communication.

Second, as long as you don't stay in your resort hotel, you can **find chances to learn about local life.** Your experience might not be as extreme as sleeping in a mountain shack with Kazakhs or sharing a Filipino's meal while surrounded by rice paddies, but if you ask around, you might discover a *Semana Santa* parade happening tomorrow or a restaurant with live flamenco dancing. If you make the effort to search and ask, you will find authentic opportunities to glimpse a day of life in that country.

Third, you might acquire new skills. Of course, you are welcome to practice the skills you have learned from previous chapters in this book (please don't touch that toilet door handle!). But you might also like to learn how to cook a *tajine* in Meknes. Or perhaps you are interested in natural textile dyes in Oaxaca. Whatever your interests are, with a little research, you might find hands-on classes in the local arts and crafts. In the very least, a guidebook or helpful hotel receptionist can point you toward tours where you can learn how gauchos ranch cattle or discover the symbolism of Sichuan Opera masks, for example.

A fourth advantage you will gain from your trip is the excitement of exploring new places. Hopefully, you won't find yourself surrounded by spider webs or in a dark alley with a swarthy sailor. If you learn from my advice in previous chapters, all your explorations should be positive experiences. But you don't have to walk a sacbe alone in the jungle or cross a glacial river on horseback to go exploring. No. Exploring can start with leaving your resort to walk down to a corner restaurant and ordering an empanada. Exploring for you might mean discovering a silent gallery in a forgotten corner of the Louvre. Whatever exploring means to you, just don't forget to do it with all your senses turned on. Smell the mangos, touch the silk, listen to the discord of the gamelan orchestra, revel in the rainbow of spices, and nibble at least one grasshopper, even if the idea is disgusting (You might like grasshoppers. They taste like shrimp!) Whatever you do, don't let the experiences of a new place pass you by.

Let's say that you didn't learn how to say "*terima kasih*." Let's imagine you never learned how to fish with cormorants, you were too shy to share Iftar (Fatoor in Morocco) with a local family, and you never strayed from the side of the Grand Canal in Venice because you were afraid of getting lost. You never ate anything "yucky," you were too stingy to buy that magnificent carpet, and you forgot to bring your camera to take photos of all the new things you saw. What a shame! In the very least, if your eyes and mind were open just halfway throughout the entire trip, hopefully, you gained one important thing: a broadened worldview.

Please tell me that you noticed life in that country you visited is not like it is back home. (You won't notice this if you never left the Xcaret Resort.) Maybe they don't do things the way they do where you live. Meat and potatoes may not be the staple diet, and not everyone drives a car. Maybe all the shops are closed from midday to 3 p.m. and everyone eats supper at 10 p.m. Perhaps the language sounded funny, and their fashion sense was not to your liking.

Despite all the differences, I pray that on your journey you realized that we are all humans. We all work and struggle, love and cry. We all must eat and drink and sleep. We raise families and say our final good byes to loved ones. Our skin tones might differ, but our blood is red. Our respective languages may be incomprehensible, but a smile is understood by everyone. Our essential humanness should draw us together. Remember—they aren't weird or wrong in their customs and culture, they are just different. Their means are different, but our ends are the same: to laugh, to love, to live.

Having a broad worldview means not only acknowledging the differences among people, but celebrating and enjoying them. It means realizing the blessings you have that others don't and gracefully accepting the blessings others can give that you lack. The wealth of human variety makes this planet a vibrant, throbbing, intriguing world.

Now go out and see it!

APPENDIX

Travel Budgeting Resources

1. **https://www.airtreks.com/ready/how-to-save-money-for-a-rtw-trip/**

20 practical tips on how to save money for your round-the word trip.

2. **http://www.budgetyourtrip.com/**

This website calculates cost of living for travel in various countries around the world. Cost of living is divided into categories such as accommodation, food, water, local transportation and entertainment for solo or couple travelers, from one-week holidays to one month and in three different travel styles—budget, mid-range and luxury.

3. **TrekHard.com Travel Calculator**
   https://tinyurl.com/yafoz85n

Sliding rules related to food, lodging, transportation styles and how often you change locations which add up your daily costs in 77 different countries.

4. **Trail Wallet**
   http://voyagetravelapps.com/trail-wallet/

A daily travel expense tracking app for iPhone and iPad.

5. **Trabee Pocket   https://trabeepocket.com/**

Similar to Trail Wallet with the added benefits of multi-currency support, customized spending categories and a travel expense report. Compatible with iOS and Android.

Airline Booking Resources

1. **www.kayak.com**

This airfare search engine has always found me the best deals. It is a one-stop site that searches airline websites and all the usuals like Expedia, Orbitz, OneTravel, Travelocity for the lowest fares possible.

2. **Trip Savvy's Guide to Budget Airlines Around the World: https://tinyurl.com/ycrzf9rr**

3. **The World's Best Low-Cost Airlines according to Skytrax World Airline Awards: https://tinyurl.com/y895p583**

Accommodation Resources

1. **Booking.com**

More and more hotels worldwide are advertising their accommodation on this site. Often you can reserve a room without paying in advance. Only a credit card number is needed to make the reservation which can often be cancelled within 48 hours of the proposed date at no charge.

2. **https://www.airbnb.com/**

Book unique homes at reasonable prices and experience a city like a local. Sometimes the owner of the home is present and sometimes you will have the place to yourself.

3. **https://wwoofinternational.org/**

You provide the volunteer manual labor on a small local farm and in exchange receive food and lodging from your host.

4. **https://www.couchsurfing.com/**
Accommodation based on goodwill and trust. Both hosts and guests can be rated on their trustworthiness. You stay for free on sofas or beds or inflatable mattresses on the floor and make new friends with your host(s).

Useful Travel Blogs

These travel blogs contain all kinds of travel tips from how to start your own travel blog to choosing the best credit cards for traveling. These are expert travelers sharing their own brand of travel tips.

1. **Nomadic Matt: www.nomadicmatt.com**
2. **Expert Vagabond: https://expertvagabond.com**
3. **The Savvy Backpacker: https://thesavvybackpacker.com/**
Tips for traveling cheaply in Europe.

Travel Forums and Other Travel/Life Abroad Sites

1. **Lonely Planet's Thorn Tree Forum:
https://www.lonelyplanet.com/thorntree/welcome**
Current travel advice from travelers like you who have been where you plan to go. Just type in a destination and read their advice.

2. **Trip Advisor: https://www.tripadvisor.com/**
Reviews about practically everything travel related for any and every destination written by people who have been there. Reviews should be taken with a grain of salt.

3. **Fodor's Travel Forum:**
https://www.fodors.com/community/
Current travel advice from travelers like you who have been where you plan to go. Just type in a destination and read their advice.

4. **http://www.bootsnall.com/**
All manner of travel advice for the independent traveler. I particularly like their free 30-day tutorials about long-term travel delivered to your email inbox. Click on their "Around the World Travel" tab to find these.

5. **Transitions Abroad:**
http://www.transitionsabroad.com/
A comprehensive resource including many articles about working, living, volunteering and studying abroad written by people who have done just that.

6. **Escape Artist:** http://www.escapeartist.com/
Similar to Transitions Abroad, but focuses more on investing and retiring overseas.

7. **The Culture Shock! Book Series:**
https://www.librarything.com/series/Culture+Shock!
Learn about culture and etiquette in 95 cities and countries. Look at the book list on this site, and then buy the book you want on Amazon.

Teaching Abroad Sites

My life of travel adventure began when I took my first overseas teaching job in China. If you are interested in teaching English as a Second Language overseas, I suggest you get some training first, like the DELTA or CELTA certificates, and then check out the jobs on these sites. Language school jobs might only require that you have a Bachelor's degree and be a native English speaker. International high schools require a valid teacher's certificate. University jobs in any field often require a Master's degree or PhD.

1. **CELTA and DELTA certificates:**
   http://www.cambridgeenglish.org/teaching-english/teaching-qualifications/

2. **The International Educator:**
   https://www.tieonline.com/subscribe.cfm
   Elementary, Middle School and High School jobs requiring teacher certification in your subject area(s).

3. **ChronicleVitae:**
   https://chroniclevitae.com/job_search/new

4. **HigherEdJobs:**
   https://www.higheredjobs.com/international/

5. **Tesol.org:** http://careers.tesol.org/jobs/

6. **https://www.esljobfeed.com/**
   Scroll over "ESL Job Feeds" tab to select jobs in your country of interest.

7. **tefl.com:**
   http://www.tefl.com/job-seeker/search.html

8. **TEFL.net:** https://www.tefl.net/esl-jobs/

ACKNOWLEDGMENTS

Thanks go first of all to my friend and savior Jesus Christ for protecting me and guiding me throughout this adventure called life. In every country I've lived, God has provided new friends to replace the family and friends I left behind. In the **U.S.A**: Sarah, thanks for being my "longest" friend ever and for welcoming me to the family of your youth group. Without the love and acceptance from you and all my youth group friends (Carl, Todd and Rachel included) I could never have survived middle school and high school. Tami, thanks for being my biggest fan and worrier. Thanks for praying for me and for making me feel like part of your family. Mary Anne, thanks for all the good conversations while we worked and for caring about and praying for me all these years. In **China**: Many, many thanks to Claire for all your help. My brother and good friend Kevin, we've been on so many great adventures; may they continue. Jeff and Bonney, thanks for being loving friends and fun travel partners. In **Slovakia**: Arjenna, I'm so glad we met, and thanks for joining me on our trip to Egypt. In **Morocco**: I can never repay you, Thomas and Fazia, for being my family and for all the walks, talks and food. In **Indonesia**: Thank you, Jos and Ossi for welcoming me to Cita Hati, your ICA home-group and for inviting me to Hadi's mountain biking club. In **Jeju, South Korea:** I'm glad I had you, Steve, to share my motorcycle and hiking adventures with. **To all my students:** You are the reason I kept on teaching. Thank you for making my job so enjoyable. And to all those unnamed who have touched my life in many small yet significant ways, I thank you.

Made in the USA
San Bernardino, CA
10 December 2017